D0036162

Pocket
MILAN & THE LAKES

TOP SIGHTS • LOCAL LIFE • MADE EASY

Paula Hardy

Jan 2016

In This Book

QuickStart Guide

Your keys to understanding the city – we help you decide what to do and how to do it

Need to Know
Tips for a smooth trip

Neighbourhoods
What's where

Explore Milan & the Lakes

The best things to see and do, neighbourhood by neighbourhood

Top Sights
Make the most of your visit

Local Life
The insider's city

The Best of Milan & the Lakes

The city's highlights in handy lists to help you plan

Best Walks
See the city on foot

Milan & the Lakes' Best...
The best experiences

Survival Guide

Tips and tricks for a seamless, hassle-free city experience

Getting Around
Travel like a local

Essential Information
Including where to stay

Our selection of the city's best places to eat, drink and experience:

◎ **Sights**

✖ **Eating**

◓ **Drinking**

✪ **Entertainment**

🔒 **Shopping**

These symbols give you the vital information for each listing:

🕽 Telephone Numbers	👪 Family-Friendly
⏱ Opening Hours	🐾 Pet-Friendly
🅿 Parking	🚌 Bus
⊘ Nonsmoking	⛴ Ferry
@ Internet Access	Ⓜ Metro
📶 Wi-Fi Access	Ⓢ Subway
🍴 Vegetarian Selection	🚋 Tram
📖 English-Language Menu	🚆 Train

Find each listing quickly on maps for each neighbourhood:

Bar Hemingway

16 ◓ Map p233, B2

Legend has it that Hemi
self, wielding a machine
rate this timber-pan
ered bar during
showpiece is a
en by Papa ar
town. Dress
s.com; Hôtel Rit
⏱6.30pm-2a

Lonely Planet's Milan & the Lakes

Lonely Planet Pocket Guides are designed to get you straight to the heart of the city.

Inside you'll find all the must-see sights, plus tips to make your visit to each one really memorable. We've split the city into easy-to-navigate neighbourhoods and provided clear maps so you'll find your way around with ease. Our expert authors have searched out the best of the city: walks, food, nightlife and shopping, to name a few. Because you want to explore, our 'Local Life' pages will take you to some of the most exciting areas to experience the real Milan & the Lakes.

And of course you'll find all the practical tips you need for a smooth trip: itineraries for short visits, how to get around, and how much to tip the guy who serves you a drink at the end of a long day's exploration.

It's your guarantee of a really great experience.

Our Promise

You can trust our travel information because Lonely Planet authors visit the places we write about, each and every edition. We never accept freebies for positive coverage, so you can rely on us to tell it like it is.

QuickStart Guide 7

Explore Milan & the Lakes 21

Worth a Trip:

QuickStart Guide

Welcome to Milan & the Lakes

Milan is Italy's city of the future, a fast-paced metropolis where creativity is big business, looking good is compulsory and after-work drinks – known as *aperitivi* – are an art form. It's also a city with ancient roots and extraordinary treasures that you'll get to experience without the usual queues. On the weekend, join the urban exodus to the elegant towns and tiered gardens of the Italian lakes.

Duomo (p24)
RICHARD I'ANSON / GETTY IMAGES ©

Milan & the Lakes
Top Sights

Duomo (p24)

With its ageless marble facade and countless pinnacles and spires piercing the sky, Milan's splendid Gothic cathedral is a veritable outdoor sculpture museum.

TIBOR BOGNAR / ROBERT HARDING ©

The Last Supper
(p80)

Saved from WWII bombs by a bank of sandbags, Leonardo da Vinci's *The Last Supper* (Il Cenacolo), painted on the refectory wall of Santa Maria delle Grazie, is one of the world's most iconic images.

Isole Borromee
(p106)

In Lago Maggiore's most beautiful corner, the Borromean Islands harbour the spectacular, privately owned palaces of the Borromei family. Palazzo Borromeo is the centrepiece, with 10 tiers of terraced gardens.

Bellagio (p116)

Wander Bellagio's zigzagging streets and rhododendron-filled gardens, then sit lakeside and while away the afternoon with a bottle of Mamete Prevostini Opera Bianco. Surely life doesn't get any better?

WORLDPHOTOS / ALAMY ©

WALTER BIBIKOW / GETTY IMAGES ©

M. GEBICKI / GETTY IMAGES ©

Pinacoteca di Brera (p58)

Founded in the 18th century alongside Italy's most prestigious art academy, the Pinacoteca houses a priceless collection of Old Master paintings that includes the likes of Titian, Tintoretto, Veronese and the Bellini brothers.

Museo del Novecento (p28)

Milan's stunning collection of 20th-century art is fittingly housed in the remodelled 1950s Palazzo dell'Arengario, which features bas-reliefs by Arturo Martini.

Museo Poldi Pezzoli (p40)

Gian Giacomo Poldi Pezzoli's historically themed apartments, decorated with his priceless collection of Renaissance paintings and artefacts, offer a unique preserved-in-amber insight into the heyday of 19th-century patronage.

REDA & CO SRL / ALAMY ©

RICHARD I'ANSON / GETTY IMAGES ©

Castello Sforzesco (p56)

Long-time seat and residence of the dukes of Milan, the Sforza castle is one of the biggest citadels in Europe, with 12 sturdy bastions and walls that once ran 3.5km. It now houses the city's civic museums.

Milan & the Lakes Local Life

Insider tips to help you find the real city

It's true the Milanese don't always have time to play nice for visitors – they're simply too busy redesigning the world. But if you're prepared to jump in, they'll happily share their intoxicating round of pursuits, be that precision shopping, browsing contemporary galleries, or loading up a plate with local delicacies while downing an expertly mixed negroni.

Shop Like a Local (p42)

▶ Fashion boutiques
▶ Historic *palazzi*

With more than 500 fashion marques crammed into 6000 sq metres of cobbled laneways, the Quadrilatero d'Oro is high-fashion theatre at its best. Names such as Armani, Bulgari and D&G are known the world over, and the Quad is also home to historic house museums, gourmet eateries and luxurious spas.

Zona Tortona (p88)

▶ Designer studios
▶ Design fair hot spot

Lying across Graffiti Bridge and behind the railway tracks of Porta Genova, the Zona Tortona was once a tangle of working-class tenements and factories. Now an area flush with studios, fashion HQs and Armani's new legacy museum, this is the place to glimpse Milan's latest ideas.

Life on the Canals (p92)

▶ Markets
▶ *Aperitivo* bars

Milan was once defined by its network of canals, which fell into disuse in the 20th century. Today the banks of the Naviglio Grande and Naviglio Pavese are lined with some of the city's best bars, clubs and artists' workshops. At weekends locals flock here for markets and sunny strolls.

Porta Romana (p102)

▶ Traditional dining
▶ Family fun

Porta Romana is one of Milan's historic districts, filled with prestigious offices, embassies and the grand *palazzi* (mansions)homes of the Milanese elite. It's full of authentic trattorias and family-friendly attractions, and is one of the city's nightlife zones, catering to students from Bocconi, Milan's business and economics university.

Navigli (p90)

Restaurants on the bank of Naviglio Grande (p93)

Other great ways to experience the city like a local:

Art Nouveau Architecture (p50)

Antica Barbieria Colla (p37)

Parco Sempione (p64)

Clooney's Como (p120)

Aperitivo (p97)

San Siro Stadium (p84)

Milanese Sushi (p66)

Bulgari Hotel (p68)

Il Gatto Nero (p125)

Chinatown (p76)

Milan & the Lakes
Day Planner

Day One

☀ If you only have one day in Milan focus on the major sites. Rise early and grab a coffee and brioche at **Giacomo Caffè** (p35) before climbing to the roof of the **Duomo** (p24) for a bird's-eye view of the city. Then head into the **Museo del Novecento** (p28) for a blast of 20th-century art. Midmorning, break for *spritz* (a type of cocktail made with prosecco) on the terrace of **Terrazza Aperol** (p35) overlooking the Duomo's extravagant spires.

☀ Window-shop down the **Galleria Vittorio Emanuele II** (p31), and for lunch choose local favourite **Trattoria Milanese** (p33) or fashion-forward **Café Trussardi** (p34). Afterwards, make for the imposing **Castello Sforzesco** (p56) to nip round the ducal apartments and admire Michelangelo's moving *Rondanini Pietà*, his last work. Relax with *aperitivo* (see p97) in Parco Sempione, on the terrace of **Bar Bianco** (p128).

☾ With prebooked tickets in hand, head for an evening tour of Leonardo da Vinci's **The Last Supper** (p80), before sliding into the bosky courtyard garden of **La Brisa** (p84) for a romantic dinner.

Day Two

☀ Coffee at **Cova** (p130) in the Quad should start your second day. Then wander the high-fashion lanes, marvelling at window displays and buying small treats such as jewel-coloured gloves from **Sermoneta** (p53) or striking fashion jewellery at **Pellini** (p50). End up on Via Manzoni at the aristocratic home of **Gian Giacomo Poldi Pezzoli** (p40) and tour the lavish interiors hung with priceless Renaissance artworks.

☀ Lunch in the cloister of elegant **La Veranda** (p43) or at historical **Bagutta** (p45). Head to Via Mozart and duck behind the high walls of modernist **Villa Necchi Campiglio** (p46) to see how aristocrats Nedda and Gigina Necchi lived in the 1930s. The house is full of delightful quotidian details: their monogrammed hairbrushes and luggage, kitchen cupboards full of crockery, and silk evening frocks hanging at the ready for evenings at **Teatro alla Scala** (La Scala; p35).

☾ Hop on tram 9 and whizz down to Navigli to join the throng of Milanese gathering for sunset *aperitivo*. Bar hop from **Mag Café** (p97) to **Ugo** (p97) and **Bar Rita** (p97), before dining at Slow Food–recommended **Le Vigne** (p96) and catching some blues at **Nibada Theatre** (p99).

Short on time?
We've arranged Milan & the Lakes' must-sees into these day-by-day itineraries to make sure you see the very best of the region in the time you have available.

Day Three

☀ Wherever you're based, make a pilgrimage to **Gattullo** (p92) for breakfast of cream-filled *sfogliatella* (sweetened ricotta pastry) and wild-strawberry tarts. Then head west for a morning exploring the **Museo Nazionale della Scienza e Tecnologia** (p83), whipping around the many medieval treasures at the **Basilica di Sant'Ambrogio** (p83) on your way. Between Leonardo's model machines and 17th-century Venetian astrolabes, take a break for a gourmet sandwich at **De Santis** (p84).

☀ After lunch, ponder Bernardino Luini's fresco cycle at the **Chiesa di San Maurizio** (p83) and see who can spot the most tortured saint. From there, head north to examine Milan's design pedigree at the **Triennale di Milano** (p63). If it's sunny, climb the **Torre Branca** (p63) for 360-degree views of Parco Sempione, then head to the **Arco della Pace** (p63) for *aperitivo* at one of the bars that ring its base.

☽ Finish the day in Brera's pretty cobbled laneways with a Milanese feast at **Ristorante Solferino** (p65) or the charming **Latteria di San Marco** (p65).

Day Four

☀ Head out of the city on the train to Como and wander the mansion-lined **Passegiata Lino Gelpi** (p120) to **Villa Olmo** (p120) for a blockbuster art show. Alternatively, head to Stresa on Lago Maggiore, where you can hop on the hydrofoil to the **Isole Borromee** (p106) to explore one of the lavish Borromean palaces and gardens. Lunch on traditional lake specialities at either **Ristorante Il Vicoletto** (p110) in Stresa or **Natta Café** (p122) in Como.

☀ In the afternoon, relax – you're on holiday! Wander the hothouses and picnic amid tulips and camellias at Lago Maggiore's **Villa Taranto** (p111), or take a quick Como hydrofoil to **Bellagio** (p116). In Bellagio you can lounge by the lake at the **lido** (p117) or take a cruise in one of **Barindelli's** (p117) seriously sexy cigarette boats.

☽ Tired and happy, take the train back to Milan and wrap things up with memorable cocktails, mixed with vintage liqueurs, and delicious sushi *aperitivo* at the **Bulgari Hotel** (p68).

Need to Know

**For more information,
see Survival Guide (p143)**

Currency
Euro (€)

Language
Italian

Visas
Generally not required for stays of up to
three months.

Money
ATMs are widely available. Credit cards
accepted in most restaurants and hotels.

Mobile Phones
Local SIM cards can be used in European
and Australian phones. Other phones must
be set to roaming.

Time
Central European Time (GMT plus one hour)

Plugs & Adaptors
Italy uses plugs with two or three round pins.
The electric current is 220V, 50Hz, but older
buildings may still use 125V.

Tipping
In restaurants leave a 10% tip if there is
no service charge. In bars, small change
is sufficient (€0.10 or €0.20). Tipping taxi
drivers is not common practice.

① Before You Go

Your Daily Budget

Budget less than €110

► Dorm beds €20–€35

► Self-catering at markets and delis

► *Aperitivo* cocktail and all-you-can-eat
buffet €8–€20

Midrange €110–€200

► Double room in a hotel €110–€200

► Two-course lunch with wine in local trattorias €25–€45

Top End more than €200

► Double room in a four-star hotel €200–€800

► Gourmet dinner in Michelin-starred
restaurant €150

► Good seats at Teatro alla Scala opera
€85–€210

Useful Websites

Lonely Planet (www.lonelyplanet.com/milan)
Destination information, bookings and more.

Milan City Tourism (www.turismo.milano.it)
Milan's official tourism portal.

Vivimilano (www.vivimilano.it) Restaurant
and cultural listings from *Corriere della Sera*.

Advance Planning

Three months before Book tickets for *The
Last Supper* and Teatro alla Scala; if visit-
ing during Fashion Week or the Salone del
Mobile, book your hotel.

One month before Book tables at top restaurants, football tickets and appointments
for bespoke tailoring.

One week before Get on guest lists for
popular club nights; see www.vivimilano.it
for gallery openings; arrange dry cleaning
(scruffy won't do).

② Arriving in Milan

Most visitors to Milan and the lakes arrive via international airports Malpensa or Linate, or through the main train station, Stazione Centrale. Public transport and private taxis are available from each hub. The Malpensa Express train links to Stazione Centrale and Cadorna.

✈ From Milan Malpensa

Destination	Best Transport
Piazza del Duomo	Malpensa Express to Stazione Centrale, M3 metro line to Duomo
Parco Sempione	Malpensa Express to Cadorna
Navigli	Malpensa Express to Cadorna, M2 metro line to Porta Genova
Lago Maggiore	Malpensa Express to Stazione Centrale, connecting train to Stresa
Lago di Como	Malpensa Express to Cadorna, connecting train to Como Nord Lago (Stazione FNM)

✈ From Milan Linate

Destination	Best Transport
Piazza del Duomo	ATM city bus to Piazza San Babila, M1 metro line to Duomo
Quadrilatero d'Oro	ATM city bus or taxi to Piazza San Babila
Navigli	ATM city bus to Piazza Risorgimento, tram 9 to Porta Genova
Lago Maggiore	Taxi or city bus to Stazione Centrale, connecting train to Stresa

③ Getting Around

Milan's public-transport system is affordable and efficient. Most visitors will get everywhere they need to go by walking, taking the metro or hopping on a tram. The unlimited one-/two-day tickets for bus, tram and metro are the best value for money.

Ⓜ Metro

Milan's metro consists of four underground lines (red M1, green M2, yellow M3, lilac M5) and the blue suburban line, the Passante Ferroviario. The metro runs from 6am to 12.30am. A ticket costs €1.50 and is valid for one metro ride or up to 90 minutes' travel on ATM buses and trams. An unlimited one-/two-day ticket on public transport costs €4.50/8.25. Tickets are sold at metro stations, tobacconists and newspaper stands.

🚋 Tram

Milan's trams range from beloved, rattling early-20th-century orange cars to modern light-rail vehicles, and criss-cross and circle the city. Trams run similar hours to the metro and tickets must be prepurchased and validated when boarding. Important tram lines to remember: 1, 2 and 3 (all running to the Duomo); 9 (circling the city to Porta Genova); and 29 and 30 (serving the middle ring road and Porta Venezia).

🚕 Taxi

Taxis are only available at designated taxi ranks; you cannot flag them down. Alternatively, phone 📞02 40 40, 📞02 69 69 or 📞02 85 85. Be aware that meters are on from the receipt of call, not from pick up. The average short city ride costs €10.

Milan & the Lakes
Neighbourhoods

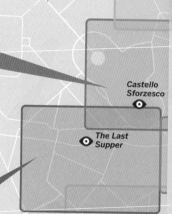

Brera & Parco Sempione (p54)
Brera's cute shops, art galleries and boho raffishness contrast with the grandeur of Castello Sforzesco and the Triennale design museum.

◉ Top Sights

Castello Sforzesco

Pinacoteca di Brera

Corso Magenta & Sant'Ambrogio (p78)
A warren of medieval streets surrounds the Basilica di Sant'Ambrogio, while Corso Magenta is lined by patrician palaces.

◉ Top Sights

The Last Supper

Navigli (p90)
The south of the city is bisected by canals and is where the hipster kids come to shop, drink and party.

Castello Sforzesco ◉

The Last Supper ◉

Porta Garibaldi & Isola (p70)
Porta Nuova's shiny skyscrapers and buzzing Corso Garibaldi are showpieces for modern Milan. In their shadow up-and-coming Isola has a cool, multicultural vibe.

Quadrilatero d'Oro & Giardini Pubblici (p38)
Milan's luxury enclave contains cobbled streets filled with high-fashion theatre, flanked by a pretty pleasure garden.

⊙ Top Sights
Museo Poldi Pezzoli

Lago Maggiore & Around (p104)
Grand villas and extraordinary gardens line Lago Maggiore, which also boasts a comfortable, mild climate.

⊙ Top Sights
Isole Borromee

Duomo & Around (p22)
Milan's historic hub is dominated by the twin temples of the Duomo and the Galleria Vittorio Emanuele II.

⊙ Top Sights
Duomo

Museo del Novecento

Lago di Como & Around (p114)
Lago di Como is scattered with charming villages, including delightful Bellagio.

⊙ Top Sights
Bellagio

Pinacoteca di Brera ⊙

Museo Poldi Pezzoli ⊙

⊙ Duomo

⊙ Museo del Novecento

Explore
Milan & the Lakes

Galleria Vittorio Emanuele II (p31)
PAOLO CORDELLI / GETTY IMAGES ©

Explore

Duomo & Around

Milan's centre is conveniently compact. The splendid cathedral sits in a vast piazza that throngs with tourists and touts. From here, choose God or Mammon, art or music, or take in all four at the Galleria Vittorio Emanuele II, Teatro alla Scala opera house, and the galleries of Palazzo Reale and Gallerie d'Italia.

The Sights in a Day

☀ Head to the **Duomo** (p24) early for sublime morning light through the stained-glass windows and a stroll around the gargoyled parapets. If it's sunny you may be able to spy the Alps over the rooftops. Break for a mid-morning *spritz* (a type of cocktail made with prosecco) at **Terrazza Aperol** (p35) and then check out the exhibition at the **Palazzo Reale** (p31).

☀ For lunch tuck into saffron risotto at **Trattoria Milanese** (p33), before immersing yourself in Milan's modernist showcase at the **Museo del Novecento** (p28) or the 18th- and 19th-century Lombard painting at the grand **Gallerie d'Italia** (p32). Afterwards, refuel with a coffee at **Giacomo Caffè** (p35) before checking out Bramante's clever optical illusion in the **Chiesa di Santa Maria Presso di San Satiro** (p32). It will then be time to join the throngs window-browsing in the **Galleria Vittorio Emanuele II** (p31).

☾ Finish the day with cocktails at **Camparino** (p34) or wine tasting at **SignorVino** (p35), and consider checking out what's on at the **Piccolo Teatro** (p36). Opera and ballet fans will need to plan ahead for a night at **Teatro alla Scala** (p35).

👁 Top Sights

Duomo (p24)

Museo del Novecento (p28)

♥ Best of Milan

History
Duomo (p24)

Biblioteca Ambrosiana (p32)

Gallerie d'Italia (p32)

Eating
Cracco (p33)

Trattoria Milanese (p33)

Culture
Palazzo Reale (p31)

Teatro alla Scala (p35)

Piccolo Teatro Grassi (p36)

Getting There

Ⓜ **Metro** Take the east–west red line (M1) for Duomo, which brings you out in front of the cathedral. The north–south yellow line (M3) also connects here from the Stazione Centrale.

🚊 **Tram** Numerous trams stop at Piazza Duomo; the most useful are trams 1, 2, 3, 15 and 9.

Top Sights
Duomo

A vision in pink Candoglia marble, Milan's cathedral aptly reflects the city's creative brio and ambition. Begun by Giangaleazzo Visconti in 1387, its design was originally considered unfeasible. Canals had to be dug to transport the vast quantities of marble to the city centre, and new technologies were invented to cater for the never-before-attempted scale. Now its pearly white facade rises like the filigree of a fairy-tale tiara, and wows the crowds with its extravagant details.

👁 Map p30, C3

www.duomomilano.it

Piazza del Duomo

roof stairs/lift €8/13

🕐 duomo 7am-6.40pm, roof terraces 9am-6.30pm, battistero 10am-6pm Tue-Sun

Ⓜ Duomo

Duomo interior

Don't Miss

The Exterior

During his stint as king of Italy, Napoleon offered to fund the Duomo's completion in 1805, in time for his coronation. The architect piled on the neo-Gothic details, a homage to the original design that displayed a prescient use of fashion logic – ie everything old is new again. The petrified pinnacles, cusps, buttresses, arches and more than 3000 statues are almost all products of the 19th century.

Roof Terraces & Lantern

Climb to the roof terraces where you'll be within touching distance of the elaborate 135 spires and their forest of flying buttresses. In the centre of the roof rises the 15th-century octagonal lantern and spire, on top of which is the golden *Madonnina* (erected in 1774). For centuries she was the highest point in the city (108.5m) until the Pirelli skyscraper outdid her in 1958.

The Interior

Initially designed to accommodate Milan's then-population of around 40,000, the cathedral's elegant, hysterical and sublimely spiritual architecture can transport 21st-century types back to a medieval mindset. Once your eyes have adjusted to the subdued light and surreal proportions inside (there are five grandiose naves supported by 52 columns), stare up, and up, to the largest stained-glass windows in Christendom.

The Floors

Before you wander among the cathedral's many treasures, look down and marvel at the polychrome marble floor that sweeps across 12,000 sq metres. The design was conceived of by Pellegrino Tibaldi and took 400 years to complete. The pink and white blocks of Candoglia marble came

☑ Top Tips

▶ Hours for the treasury, crypt, baptistry and roof vary, so check the website for details.

▶ The €13 combination ticket for the roof terraces, baptistry and treasury is a good deal.

▶ It's quicker to ascend to the roof via the 165 steps rather than the tiny elevator, which attracts a long queue.

▶ It's possible to take pictures inside the Duomo if you purchase a special photography ticket (€2).

✄ Take a Break

Nip into Giacomo Caffe (p35) for coffee or head to the sun-trap terrace of Terrazza Aperol (p35) for a midmorning *spritz*.

Continue on the traditional theme with lunch at Trattoria Milanese (p33).

from the cathedral's own quarries at Mergozzo (bequeathed in perpetuity by Giangaleazzo), and are inlaid with black marble from Varenna and red marble from Arzo.

The Sun Dial

On the floor by the main entrance you may notice a brass strip lined with signs of the zodiac. This is, in fact, an 18th-century sundial, installed by astronomers from the Accademia di Brera in 1768. A hole in the vault of the south aisle casts a ray of sunlight at various points along its length (depending on the season) at astronomical noon. The device was so precise that all the city's clocks were set by it up until the 19th century.

St Bartholomew

One of the cathedral's more unusual statues is the 1562 figure of St Bartholomew by Marco d'Agrate, a student of Leonardo da Vinci. It depicts St Bartholomew post-torture with his skin flayed from his flesh and cast about his neck like a cape. For 16th-century sculptors he was a favourite subject, enabling them to show off their anatomical knowledge as well as their technique.

The Transept

Bisecting the nave, the transept is especially rich in works of art. At either end there is an altar decorated with polychrome marbles, the most elaborate being the *Altar to the Virgin of the Tree* on the north side. In front of this stands the monumental, 5m-high

Milan Duomo

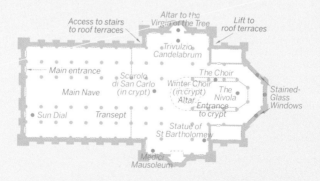

Access to stairs to roof terraces

Altar to the Virgin of the Tree

Lift to roof terraces

Trivulzio Candelabrum

Main entrance

Scurolo di San Carlo (in crypt)

The Choir

Winter Choir (in crypt)
Altar

The Nivola

Stained-Glass Windows

Main Nave

Entrance to crypt

Sun Dial

Transept

Statue of St Bartholomew

Medici Mausoleum

Trivulzio candelabrum, a masterpiece of medieval bronze work, its seven branches inset with precious stones.

The Choir

Completed in 1614, the sculpted choir stalls were designed by Pellegrino Tibaldi and carved by Paolo de'Gazzi, Virgilio del Conte and the Taurini brothers. The three tiers of sculpture represent the life of Milanese bishops Anatalone and Galdino at the base, the martyred saints in the centre and the life of St Ambrose above.

The Nivola

High up in the apse, a red light signifies the location of the cathedral's most precious relic: a nail said to be from Christ's cross. During the annual Feast of the Exaltation of the Cross (Saturday closest to the 14th September), the archbishop ascends to the roof in a *nivola* (decorated basket) and the relic is put on display for three days.

The Crypt

From the ambulatory that encircles the choir are the stairs down to the crypt or Winter Choir. Designed by Tibaldi, this jewel-like circular chapel with its red porphyry pillars, polychrome marble floor and stucco ceiling contains a casket holding the relics of various saints and martyrs. A wooden choir stall encircles the room.

Scurolo di San Carlo

Through a gap in the crypt's choir stalls, a dark corridor leads to a

Duomo rooftop

memorial chapel housing the remains of saintly Carlo Borromeo (cardinal archbishop of Milan; 1564–84), contained in a rock-crystal casket atop a silver altar.

Veneranda Fabbrica del Duomo

The epic building of Milan's cathedral necessitated the creation of a 'factory' for all operational activities and maintenance. The Fabbrica del Duomo oversaw construction from 1387 until the last gate was inaugurated in 1965. Today it continues the work of restoring and maintaining the cathedral. It's possible to visit the Fabbrica's marble quarries at Lago di Mergozzo, near Lago Maggiore.

Top Sights
Museo del Novecento

Overlooking Piazza del Duomo, with fabulous views of the cathedral, Mussolini's Palazzo dell'Arengario is where he would harangue huge crowds in the glory days of his regime. It's now home to Milan's museum of 20th-century art. Built around a futuristic spiral ramp (an ode to the Guggenheim), the museum's lower floors are cramped, but the heady collection, which includes the likes of Boccioni, Campigli, Giorgio de Chirico and Marinetti, more than distracts.

Map p30, C3

www.museodelnovecento.org

Via Marconi 1

adult/reduced €5/3

2.30-7.30pm Mon, 9.30am-7.30pm Tue, Wed, Fri & Sun, to 10.30pm Thu & Sat

M Duomo

Museo del Novecento interior

Don't Miss

Palazzo dell'Arengario

The austere Arengario consists of two symmetrical buildings each with a three-tier arcaded facade. It was built in the 1950s by star architects Piero Portaluppi, Giovanni Muzio, Pier Giulio Magristretti and Enrico Griffini, and is decorated with bas-reliefs by Milanese sculptor Arturo Martini, who's work now features in the museum's collection. The name *arengario* comes from the building's original function as the government seat during the Fascist period, when officials would *arringa* (harangue) the local populous from the building's balcony.

The Collection

The museum's permanent collection is an ode to 20th-century modern art, and has a particular focus on Milanese home-grown talent. Chronological rooms take you from Volpedo's powerful neo-Impressionist painting of striking workers, *Il Quarto Stato* (The Fourth Estate; 1901), through the dynamic work of futurist greats such as Umberto Boccioni, Carlo Carra, Gino Severini and Giacomo Balla, then on to abstractism, surrealism, spatialism and Arte Povera. The collection provides a fascinating social commentary on Italy's trajectory through two world wars and into the technological era.

Giacomo Arengario

The 3rd-floor **bistro** (📞 02 7209 3814; www.giacomo arengario.com; meals €50-60; 🕐 noon-midnight; ❄) overlooking the Duomo is a highlight, decorated in a luxe art deco style. Top-notch bistro fare includes fish platters, truffles and game. During the day you can gaze out at the Duomo's spires and at night enjoy the jewel-like colours of the stained-glass windows.

☑ Top Tips

▶ Consider a guided tour, available in Italian, English and French.

▶ The best views of the Duomo are to be had from the top floor, standing beneath Lucio Fontana's squiggle of fluorescent light: *Luce Spaziale: Struttura al Neon* (1951).

▶ The Arengario is linked to the Palazzo Reale (p31) by a suspended footbridge.

✕ Take a Break

Book ahead for lunch at 3rd-floor Giacomo Arengario to make sure you snag a seat on the terrace.

In the evening cross the piazza for drinks among the beautiful people at Straf Bar (p35).

Sights

Palazzo Reale
MUSEUM, PALACE

1 ◎ Map p30, C3

Empress Maria Theresa's favourite architect Giuseppe Piermarini gave this town hall and Visconti palace a neoclassical overhaul in the late 18th century. The supremely elegant interiors were all but destroyed by WWII bombs; the **Sala delle Cariatidi** remains unrenovated as a reminder of war's indiscriminate destruction. Now the once-opulent palace hosts blockbuster art exhibits attracting serious crowds to shows as diverse as Warhol, Chagall, da Vinci and Giotto. (📞 02 87 56 72; www.comune.milano.it/palazzoreale; Piazza del Duomo 12; admission varies; ⊙ exhibitions 2.30-7.30pm Mon, 9.30am-7.30pm Tue, Wed, Fri & Sun, to 10.30pm Thu & Sat; Ⓜ Duomo)

Il Grande Museo del Duomo
MUSEUM

2 ◎ Map p30, C3

Stepping through Guido Canali's glowing spaces in the Duomo's new museum is like coming upon the sets for an episode of *Game of Thrones*. Tortured gargoyles leer down through the shadows; shafts of light strike the wings of heraldic angels; and a monstrous godhead glitters awesomely in copper once intended for the high altar. It's an exciting display, masterfully choreographed through 26 rooms, which tell the 600-year story of the cathedral's construction through priceless sculptures, paintings, stained glass, tapestries and bejewelled treasures. (www.museo.duomomilano.it; Piazza del Duomo 12; adult/reduced €6/4; ⊙ 10am-6pm Tue-Sun; Ⓜ Duomo)

Galleria Vittorio Emanuele II
HISTORIC BUILDING

3 ◎ Map p30, C2

So much more than a shopping arcade, the neoclassical Galleria Vittorio Emanuele II is a soaring iron-and-glass structure known locally as *il salotto de Milano,* the city's fine drawing room. Shaped like a crucifix, it also marks the *passeggiata* (evening stroll) route from Piazza del Duomo to Piazza di Marino and the doors of Teatro alla Scala (La Scala). In 2015 a new **highline walkway** (www.highlinegalleria.com; Via Pellico 2; adult/reduced €12/10; ⊙ 9am-11pm; Ⓜ Duomo) gave access to the Galleria's rooftops for stunning

---

Understand
Superstition in the Galleria

Giuseppe Mengoni designed the Galleria Vittorio Emanuele II as a showcase for modern Milan. Tragically, he plummeted to his death from scaffolding just weeks before the 14-year project was completed in 1877. Long-standing Milanese tradition claims you can avoid his bad luck by grinding your heel into the testicles of the mosaic bull on the floor and spinning backwards three times.

bird's-eye views of the arcade and the city. (Piazza del Duomo; Ⓜ Duomo)

Gallerie d'Italia
MUSEUM

4 Map p30, C1

Housed in three fabulously decorated palaces, the enormous art collection of Fondazione Cariplo and Intesa Sanpaolo bank pays homage to 18th- and 19th-century Lombard painting. From a magnificent sequence of bas-reliefs by Antonio Canova to luminous Romantic masterpieces by Francesco Hayez, the works span 23 rooms and document Milan's significant contribution to the rebirth of Italian sculpture, the patriotic romanticism of the Risorgimento (reunification period) and the birth of futurism at the dawn of the 20th century. (www.gallerieditalia.com; Piazza della Scala 6; adult/reduced €10/8; ⊘9.30am-7.30pm Tue-Sun; Ⓜ Duomo)

Palazzo della Ragione
GALLERY

5 Map p30, B3

Erected between 1228 and 1251, Milan's Palace of Reason is one of the few remaining medieval constructions to survive. Its Romanesque arcade served as a marketplace, auction site and public assembly while justice was dispensed upstairs in a large frescoed hall. Now restored, the space (sans frescoes) is devoted to temporary contemporary-photography exhibitions. (Broletto Nuovo; www.palazzodellaragionefotografia.it; Piazza dei Mercanti; adult/reduced €12/10; ⊘9.30am-8.30pm Tue, Wed, Fri & Sun, to 10.30pm Thu & Sat; Ⓜ Duomo)

Biblioteca e Pinacoteca Ambrosiana
GALLERY, LIBRARY

6 Map p30, A3

Europe's first public library, built in 1609, the Biblioteca Ambrosiana was more a symbol of intellectual ferment than of quiet scholarship. It houses more than 75,000 volumes and 35,000 manuscripts including Leonardo da Vinci's priceless collection of drawings, the *Atlantic Codex*. An art gallery – the Pinacoteca – was added later. It exhibits Italian paintings from the 14th to the 20th century, most famously Caravaggio's *Canestra di frutta* (Basket of Fruit), which launched both his career and Italy's ultrarealist traditions. (☏ 02 80 69 21; www.ambrosiana. it; Piazza Pio XI 2; adult/reduced €15/10; ⊘10am-6pm Tue-Sun; Ⓜ Duomo)

Chiesa di Santa Maria Presso di San Satiro
CHURCH

7 Map p30, B3

Here's an escape from the Zara/Benneton/H&M maelstrom. Ludovico Sforza saw potential in this little church built on top of the 9th-century mausoleum of martyr San Satiro, and asked architect Donato Bramante to refurbish it in 1482. His ambition wasn't dampened by the project's scale: a *trompe l'œil*–coffered niche on the shallow apse makes the backdrop to the altar mimic the Pantheon in Rome. (Via Speronari 3; ⊘9.30am-5.30pm Mon-Sat, 2-5.30pm Sun; Ⓜ Duomo)

Cracco

Eating

Cracco

GASTRONOMIC €€€

 Map p30, B3

Star chef Carlo Cracco keeps the Milanese in thrall with his off-the-wall inventiveness. The *risotto al sedano, rapa, tartufo nero e caffè* (risotto with celery, turnip, black truffle and coffee) is unlike any traditional northern Italian rice dish. Let the waiters do the thinking by ordering one of the tasting menus (€130 and €160). (📞02 87 67 74; www.ristorantecracco.it; Via Victor Hugo 4; meals €130-160; 🕑7.30pm-12.30am Mon & Sat, 12.30-2.30pm & 7.30pm-12.30am Tue-Fri; Ⓜ Duomo)

Trattoria Milanese

MILANESE €€

 Map p30, A4

Like an old friend you haven't seen in years, this true trattoria welcomes you with generous goblets of wine, hearty servings of traditional Milanese fare and convivial banter over the vegetable buffet. Regulars slide into their favourite spots, barely needing to order as waiters bring them their usual: meatballs wrapped in cabbage, minestrone or the sinfully good *risotto al salto* (refried risotto). (📞02 8645 1991; Via Santa Marta 11; meals €30-45; 🕑12.30-2.30pm & 7-11.30pm; 🚊2, 14)

Café Trussardi

ITALIAN €€

10 Map p30, B2

Whether for a glass of wine and some root-vegetable crisps at the bar, or a posh lamb kebab with yoghurt and mint from the small, changing menu beneath Patrick Blanc's beautiful vertical garden in the courtyard, this is one of Milan's most stylish, low-key dining options. Upstairs, the **Trussardi alla Scala** (☑02 8068 8201; www.trussardiallascala.com; Piazza della Scala 5; menus from €140; ⏱12.30-2.30pm & 8-10.30pm Mon-Fri, 8-10.30pm Sat; ❄; M Duomo) restaurant serves Michelin-starred fare from talented chef Luigi Taglienti. (☑02 8068 8295; www.cafetrussardi.it; Piazza della Scala 5; meals €25-40; ⏱noon-12.30am; M Duomo)

Peck Italian Bar

ITALIAN €€

11 Map p30, B3

Run by the folk from historic Peck (p37) deli, this all-day restaurant appeals to a banking and business-lunch crowd. Like the clientele, the food is traditional and the service efficient. (☑02 869 30 17; www.peck.it; Via Cantù 3; meals €35-45; ⏱11.30am-9.30pm Mon-Sat; ❄; M Duomo)

Luini

FAST FOOD €

12 Map p30, C2

This historic joint is the go-to place for *panzerotti,* delicious pizza-dough parcels stuffed with a combination of mozzarella, spinach, tomato, ham or spicy salami, and then fried or baked in a wood-fired oven. (www.

luini.it; Via Santa Radegonda 16; panzerotti €2.50; ⏱10am-3pm Mon, to 8pm Tue-Sat; ❄; M Duomo)

GB Bar

SANDWICHES €

13 Map p30, C2

Big, delicious and well priced, GB's *panini* are stuffed with gourmet fillings including smoked swordfish, pulled pork, top-quality Lombard cheeses and Asti truffles. There's some outdoor seating – and a regular queue, but service is fast. (Via Agnello 18; sandwiches €4-5; ⏱6.30am-5pm Mon-Fri, to 7.30pm Sat; M Duomo)

Trattoria da Pino

MILANESE €

14 Map p30, E3

In a city full of models in Michelin-starred restaurants, working-class da Pino offers the perfect antidote. Sit elbow-to-elbow at long cafeteria-style tables and order up bowls of *bollito misto* (mixed boiled meats), hand-made pasta and curried veal nuggets. (☑02 7600 0532; Via Cerva 14; meals €20-25; ⏱noon-3pm Mon-Sat; M San Babila)

Drinking

Camparino in Galleria

BAR, CAFE

15 Map p30, C3

Open since the inauguration of the Galleria Vittorio Emanuele II shopping arcade in 1867, this perfectly preserved art nouveau bar has served drinks to the likes of Verdi, Toscanini, Dudovich and Carrà. Cast-iron chandeliers, huge mirrored walls trimmed with wall mosaics of birds and flowers set the tone for a classy Campari-based *aperitivo* (see p97). Drinks at the bar are cheaper. (www. camparino.it; Piazza del Duomo 21; drinks €12-24; ☺7.15am-8.40pm)

SignorVino
WINE BAR

16 Map p30, D3

On a mission to educate drinkers in the diversity of Italian wines, SignorVino is a wine store, bar and restaurant rolled into one. There are more than 600 bottles available to sample, and lunch and dinner menus (meals from €18 to €30) propose regional Italian dishes designed to pair with the wines. Arrive early for tables overlooking the Duomo. (☏02 8909 2539; www.signorvino. it; Piazza del Duomo; ☺8am-midnight Mon-Fri, 9am-midnight Sat & Sun; Ⓜ Duomo)

Straf Bar
BAR

17 Map p30, C2

A busy nightly *aperitivo* scene kicks on until pumpkin hour at the Straf's super-sexy hotel bar. The decor is along the now-familiar mod-exotic lines: wood, metal and stone played up against minimalist concrete. (www.straf.it; Via San Raffaele 3; ☺11am-midnight; Ⓜ Duomo)

Terrazza Aperol
BAR

18 Map p30, C3

With its whacky moulded orange bar, orange bubble lights and low-slung '70s seats, this bar dedicated to the classic Aperol *spritz* cocktail channels a strong Austin Powers vibe. Still, the Duomo's extravagant exterior, which seems within arm's reach from the terrace, is more than a match for a paisley velvet suit. (www.terrazzaaperol.it; Piazza del Duomo; cocktails €12-17; ☺11am-11pm Sun-Fri, to midnight Sat; Ⓜ Duomo)

Giacomo Caffè
CAFE

19 Map p30, C3

Tucked beneath the arches of Palazzo Reale, this period cafe with a secluded upstairs reading gallery is a good place to grab a coffee or midmorning *spritz*. The 19th-century-style bar shows off cake stands piled high with pastries, and there's a small menu of light meals and salads. (www.giacomo caffe.com; Piazza Reale 12; ☺8am-8pm; Ⓜ Duomo)

Entertainment

Teatro alla Scala
OPERA

20 Map p30, C1

One of the most famous opera stages in the world, La Scala's season runs from early December through July. You can also see theatre, ballet and concerts here year-round (except August). Buy tickets online or by phone up to two months before the performance, and then from the central **box office** (☏02 7200 3744; www. teatroallascala.org; Galleria Vittorio Emanuele II; ☺noon-6pm; Ⓜ Duomo).

When rehearsals are not in session, you can get a glimpse of the gilt-encrusted interior, or visit the **museum** (La Scala Museum; Largo Ghiringhelli 1; admission €7; ⏱9am-12.30pm & 1.30-5.30pm; MDuomo) next door. On performance days, 140 tickets for the gallery are sold two hours before the show (one ticket per customer). Queue early. (La Scala; ☑02 8 87 91; www.teatroal-lascala.org; Piazza della Scala; MDuomo)

Piccolo Teatro Grassi   THEATRE

 Map p30, A2

This risk-taking little repertory theatre was opened in 1947 by Paolo Grassi and theatre director Giorgio Strehler, who then embarked on a nationwide movement of avant-garde productions and Commedia dell'Arte revivals. Additional programming, including ballet, goes on at sibling space Piccolo Teatro Strehler (p68). (☑02 4241 1889; www.piccoloteatro.org; Via Rovello 2; MCordusio)

Shopping

Wait and See   FASHION

22 🔒 Map p30, A4

With collaborations with international brands and designers such as Missoni, Etro and Anna Molinari under her belt, Uberta Zambeletti launched her own collection in 2010. Quirky Wait and See indulges her eclectic tastes and showcases unfamiliar brands alongside items exclusively designed for the store, including super-fun Clodomiro T-shirts and Sartorio Vico knitted necklaces. (☑02 7208 0195; www. waitandsee.it; Via Santa Marta 14; ⏱3.30-7.30pm Mon, 10.30am-7.30pm Tue-Sat; MDuomo, Missori)

Moroni Gomma   HOMEWARES, ACCESSORIES

23 🔒 Map p30, D2

Stocked with irresistible gadgets and great accessories for the bathroom, kitchen and office, this family-owned design store is a one-stop shop for funky souvenirs and Milanese keepsakes. Who but the strongest willed will be able to resist the cuckoo clock shaped like the Duomo, a retro telephone in pastel colours or classic Italian moccasins in nonslip rubber? (☑02 79 62 20; www.moronigomma.it; Corso Matteotti 14; ⏱3-7pm Mon, 10am-7pm Tue-Sun; MSan Babila)

Borsalino   ACCESSORIES

24 🔒 Map p30, C2

Iconic Alessandrian milliner Borsalino has worked with design greats such as Achille Castiglioni, who once designed a pudding-bowl bowler hat. This outlet in the Galleria Vittoria Emanuele II (p31) shopping arcade stocks seasonal favourites. The main showroom is at **Via Sant'Andrea 5** (☑02 7601 7072; www.borsalino.com; Via Sant'Andrea 5; MMontenapoleone). (☑02 8901 5436; www. borsalino.com; Galleria Vittorio Emanuele II 92; ⏱3-7pm Mon, 10am-7pm Tue-Sat; MDuomo)

Peck
FOOD, WINE

25 Map p30, B3

Milan's historic deli is smaller than its reputation suggests, but what it lacks in space it makes up for in variety. It's home to a mind-boggling selection of *parmigiano reggiano* (Parmesan) and myriad other treasures: chocolates, pralines, pastries, freshly made gelato, seafood, caviar, pâté, fruit and vegetables, truffle products, olive oils and balsamic vinegars. (✍02 802 31 61; www.peck.it; Via Spadari 9; ☺3.30-7.30pm Mon, 9.30am-7.30pm Tue-Sat; Ⓜ Duomo)

Hoepli International Bookstore
BOOKS

26 Map p30, C2

Italy's largest bookshop has six floors and some 500,000 titles plus rare antiquarian books, as well as English- and German-language sections. Don't neglect to browse the Italian shelves; local publishers are known for their beautiful cover design and innovative pictorial titles. (✍02 86 48 71; www.hoepli.it; Via Ulrico Hoepli 5; ☺10am-7.30pm Mon-Sat; Ⓜ Duomo)

La Rinascente
DEPARTMENT STORE

27 Map p30, C2

Italy's most prestigious department store doesn't let the fashion capital

Ⓠ Local Life
Antica Barbieria Colla

Take a pew next to politicians, football stars and businessmen and let jovial Franco Bompieri steam, lather and close shave you into a state of bliss. Opened in 1904, **Antica Barbieria Colla** (Map p30, C1; ✍02 87 43 12; www.anticabarbieriacolla.it; Via Gerolamo Morone 3; ☺8.30am-12.30pm & 2.30-7pm Tue-Sat; Ⓜ Duomo, Ⓠ1) is the oldest barber shop in Europe – the brush once used to groom Puccini is proudly displayed – and its range of own-brand shaving creams and colognes is second to none.

down – come for Italian diffusion lines, French lovelies and LA upstarts. The basement also hides a 'Made in Italy' design supermarket, and chic hairdresser Aldo Coppola is on the top floor. Take away edible souvenirs from the 7th-floor food market (and peer across to the Duomo while you're at it). (✍02 8 85 21; www.rinascente.it; Piazza del Duomo; ☺8.30am-midnight Mon-Sat, 10am-midnight Sun; Ⓜ Duomo)

Explore

Quadrilatero d'Oro & Giardini Pubblici

Northeast of the Duomo, the Quadrilatero d'Oro (Golden Quad) sings a siren song to luxury-label lovers the world over. It also goes by the diminutive Monte Nap after Via Monte Napoleone, which is one of its defining four streets, along with Via della Spiga, Via Sant'Andrea and Via Borgospesso. To the northeast, Corso Venezia borders the Giardini Pubblici, a 19th-century pleasure garden.

The Sights in a Day

☀ Start the day with a slug of coffee and a dainty pastry at **Sant'Ambroeus** (p50), the Quad's most elegant café. Then tour the fabulous, art-filled apartment of the **Museo Poldi Pezzoli** (p40) and check out the Countess Bolognini's china and objets d'art at **Palazzo Morando** (p43). You'll need to put on your shades as you trot between the two to avoid being dazzled by the Quad's fabulous window displays of luxury goods.

☀ Come lunch time you'll be deliberating over gourmet sandwiches at **Chic & Go** (p47), exquisite Mediterranean fare in the cloister garden of **La Veranda** (p43) or a trip down memory lane at historic **Bagutta** (p45). You won't be disappointed by any of them.

☾ Satiated, head north to wander along the winding paths and around the ponds of the **Giardini Pubblici** (p45). Maybe you'll take in a photography exhibit at **PAC** (p45) or seek out the offbeat apartment of the **Casa Museo Boschi-di Stefano** (p45) for a dose of futurist art. *Aperitivo* (see p97) then beckons at **Al Bufera** (p47) and **HClub Diana** (p48) with a light vegetarian dinner at **Joia** (p46).

For shopping like a local in Quadrilatero d'Oro, see p42.

◉ Top Sights

Museo Poldi Pezzoli (p40)

◯ Local Life

Shop Like a Local (p42)

♥ Best of Milan

Art

Museo Poldi Pezzoli (p40)

Casa Museo Boschi-di Stefano (p45)

PAC (p45)

Fashion

Aspesi (p43)

Mutinelli (p51)

Doriani (p53)

Eating

La Veranda (p43)

Bagutta (p45)

Pavé (p47)

Getting There

Ⓜ **Metro** Montenapoleone, for the Quad take the yellow M3 line.

Ⓜ **Metro** For the south end of the Giardini Pubblici, exit at Palestro. For the north end exit at Porta Venezia. Both are on M1, the red line.

Ⓜ **Metro** For Corso Buenos Aires and Museo Boschi-di Stefano, continue to Lima from Porta Venezia.

Top Sights
Museo Poldi Pezzoli

Inheriting his vast fortune at the age of 24, Gian Giacomo Poldi Pezzoli also inherited his mother's love of art. During extensive European travels he was inspired by the 'house museum' that was later to become London's Victoria & Albert Museum. As his collection grew, Pezzoli had the idea of transforming his apartments into a series of historically themed rooms based on the great art periods of the past (the Middle Ages, early Renaissance, baroque and rococo). Today these Sala d'Artista are works of art in themselves.

◉ Map p30, A4

☎ 02 79 48 89

www.museopoldipezzoli.it

Via Alessandro Manzoni 12

adult/reduced €10/7

🕙 10am-6pm Wed-Mon

Ⓜ Montenapoleone

The Black Room, Museo Poldi Pezzoli

Don't Miss

Sala d'Armi

The armoury was the first room of Pezzoli's 'house museum' to be completed. Its neo-Gothic interiors were styled by Teatro alla Scala set designer Filippo Peroni, but his theatrical folly was destroyed in WWII. The new room, with its tomblike interior designed by Arnaldo Pomodoro, feels like something from a 16th-century *Raiders of the Lost Ark*.

The Grand Staircase

An impressive neobaroque staircase spirals up to the 1st-floor apartments around an extravagant fountain designed by Giuseppe Bertini. It's adorned with brass cherubs originally intended for the Portinari Chapel (p95), but Pezzoli thought they'd look good in his stairwell.

Sala d'Artista

Of the original apartment, only four themed rooms survived WWII bombs, and have been refurbished in exquisite detail: the rococo-style Stucco Room; the Black Room, originally clad in mahogany and ivory; the Antique Murano room, Pezzoli's bedroom; and the Byzantine-influenced Dante study, where Pezzoli kept his prized possessions.

The Collection

As a collector, Pezzoli focused on his passion for arms, the decorative arts and Renaissance paintings. Wander from room to room and admire Lombard Renaissance masters Foppa, Bergognone and Luini; Tuscan and Venetian greats including Botticelli, Bellini and Piero della Francesca; and the beautiful *Portrait of a Woman* by del Pollaiolo, which is now the museum's icon. Between them you'll skirt around displays of Venetian glass, 18th-century porcelain and cabinets gleaming with jewellery.

☑ Top Tips

▶ The Poldi Pezzoli is closed on Tuesdays.

▶ In addition to the Sala d'Artista, the museum has a unique collection of timepieces.

▶ Guided tours are available in a variety of languages and last about an hour.

▶ The museum is part of the Case Museo card network (p46), which offers a discount on admission to Milan's four 'house museums'.

✗ Take a Break

The museum's new 1st-floor **Pollaiolo Terrace** (⏱11am-6pm) is an impeccably tasteful place for a drink.

Follow the fashion crowd around the corner for gourmet *panini* from Chic & Go (p47). These are no ordinary sandwiches, but are stuffed with the finest ingredients money can buy.

Local Life
Shop Like a Local

For anyone interested in the fall of a frock or the cut of a jacket, a stroll around the Quadrilatero d'Oro, the world's most famous shopping district, is a must. This quaintly cobbled quadrangle of streets is full of Italy's most famous brands sporting fantastic window displays. Even if you don't have the slightest urge to sling a swag of glossy carriers over your arm, the people-watching is priceless.

1 Coffee at Cova

Coffee and cake at **Pasticceria Cova** (☎ 02 7600 5599; www.pasticceriacova.com; Via Monte Napoleone 8; ⏱ 7.30am-8.30pm Mon-Sat; Ⓜ Montenapoleone) gives you a glimpse into the world of Monte Nap. Aggressively accessorised matrons crowd the bar barking orders at the staff. This is the oldest cafe in Milan, opened in 1817 by Antonio Cova, a soldier of Napoleon.

❷ Historic Fashion

For a glimpse of aristocratic life during the 18th century, wander around **Palazzo Morando** (☑02 8846 5735; www.costumemodaimmagine.mi.it; Via Sant'Andrea 6; adult/reduced €10/8.50; ⏰9am-1pm & 2-5.30pm Tue-Sun; Ⓜ San Babila). Housing the personal collections of Countess Bolognini, the apartments are also hung with the city's civic art collection, which provides a picture of Milan as it was during the Napoleonic era.

❸ Browsing 'Monte Nap'

Via Monte Napoleone has always been synonymous with elegance and money (Napoleon's government managed loans here) and now it is the most important street of the Quad, and lined with global marques. Among the giants, classic heritage names persist, such as **Aspesi** (☑02 7602 2478; www.aspesi.com; Via Monte Napoleone 13; ⏰10am-7pm Mon-Sat; Ⓜ San Babila, Montenapoleone).

❹ Lunch at the Four Seasons

The Quad's most discreet and luxurious hotel, the Four Seasons is tucked out of sight down narrow Via Gesù. The neoclassical facade hides a 15th-century Renaissance convent complete with frescoes and a tranquil arcaded cloister. Dine here at one of the nine outdoor tables at **La Veranda** (☑02 7 70 88; www.fourseasons.com/milan; Via Gesú 6/8; meals €80-90; ⏰noon-4.30pm & 5.30-11pm; 🅿❄🐾♿; Ⓜ Montenapoleone) and savour Sergio Mei's award-winning cuisine.

❺ Museo Bagatti Valsecchi

Though born a few centuries too late, Fausto and Giuseppe Bagatti Valsecchi were determined to be Renaissance men, and from 1878 to 1887 they built their **home** (☑02 7600 6132; www.museobagattivalsecchi.org; Via Gesù 5; adult/reduced €9/6; ⏰1-5.45pm Tue, Wed & Fri-Sun, to 9pm Thu; Ⓜ Montenapoleone) as a living museum of the Quattrocento (the cultural and artistic events of 15th-century Italy). Decorated after the style of the ducal palaces in Mantua, the apartments are full of Renaissance furnishings, tapestries and paintings.

❻ Homewares on Via Manzoni

Established in Omegna in 1921, **Alessi** (☑02 79 57 26; www.alessi.com; Via Manzoni 14-16; ⏰10am-2pm & 3-7pm Mon, 10am-7pm Tue-Sat; Ⓜ Montenapoleone) has crafted more than 22,000 utensils, many of which have been designed by the world's leading architect-designers. Some pieces now reside in New York's MoMA, but you can find everything Alessi has ever done at this flagship store.

❼ Spa on Via della Spiga

Who wouldn't love shopping on pedestrianised Via della Spiga? But if the cobbles are killing your feet, take the back door into the Hotel Baglioni for a Campari and soda in the salon-style cafe or book a facial in the hotel's **Spiga 8 Spa** (☑02 4547 3111; www.baglionihotels.com; Hotel Baglioni, Via della Spiga 8; treatments from €80; ⏰10am-9pm Mon-Fri, to 7pm Sat & Sun; Ⓜ San Babila).

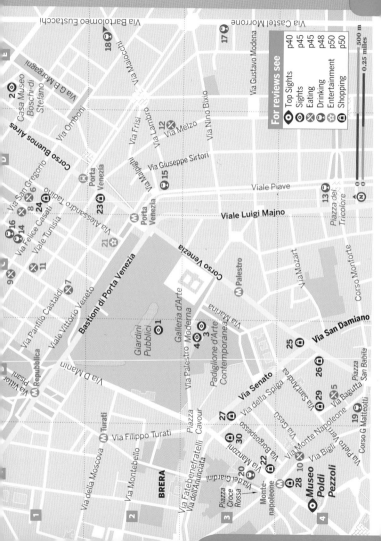

Via Bartolomeo Eustachi

Via Castel Morrone

Via G B Moreganti

Casa Museo Boschi-di Stefano 2

18

17

Via Gustavo Modena

Via Maiocchi

Via Frisi

Via Lambro

Via Melzo 12

Via Nino Bixio

Via Ombomi

Corso Buenos Aires

Via San Gregorio

Via Giuseppe Sirtori

Porta Venezia

15

Viale Piave

Via Felice Casati 24 6

23

Porta Venezia

Viale Luigi Majno 13

Piazza del Tricolore

16 14

Viale Tunisia

21

Via Alessandro Tadino

N

Via Panfilo Castaldi 7

11

9

Bastioni di Porta Venezia

Viale Vittorio Veneto

Corso Venezia

Palestro

Via Mozart

Corso Monforte

Via Vittor Pisani

Repubblica

Via D Manin

Giardini Pubblici 1

Galleria d'Arte Moderna

Via Palestro

Via Marina

Palestro

Via San Damiano

Via della Moscova

Turati

Via Filippo Turati

Padiglione d'Arte Contemporanea

Via Senato 25

Piazza San Babila

Via Montebello

Piazza Cavour

27

Via della Spiga

26

Via Santandrea

29

5

Via Gesù

Corso G Matteotti

BRERA

Via Fatebenefratelli Via dell'Annunciata

30

22

20

Via Manzoni

Via Borgospesso

Via Monte Napoleone

28

10

Via Bigli

19

Corso G Matteotti

Piazza Croce Rossa

Monte napoleone

Museo Poldi Pezzoli

Via del Giardini

Via Pietro Verri

For reviews see

◉ Top Sights		p40
◎ Sights		p45
✗ Eating		p45
◔ Drinking		p48
✿ Entertainment		p50
◉ Shopping		p50

500 m
0.25 miles

Sights

Giardini Pubblici
GARDENS

1 ⊙ Map p44, B2

A life story unfolds as you follow pebble paths past bumper cars and a carousel, onwards past games of kick-to-kick, kissing teens, a beer kiosk, babies in prams, jogging paths and shady benches. Jump in, or just stop and smell the roses. For grey days the neo-Romanesque **Museo Civico di Storia Naturale** (Natural History Museum; ☑02 8846 3337; Corso Venezia 55; adult/reduced €5/3; ⊗9am-5.30pm Tue-Sun; ☝; MPalestro) beckons families with quaint displays and dioramas of dinosaurs, fossils, fauna and the largest geology collection in Europe. (⊗6.30am-sunset; MPalestro)

Casa Museo Boschi-di Stefano
MUSEUM

2 ⊙ Map p44, E1

Milan's most eccentric museum of 20th-century Italian painting is crowded in a 1930s apartment that still has the appearance of the haute-bourgeois home it once was. It's a heady art hit, with Boccioni's dynamic brushstrokes propelling painting towards futurism; the nostalgically metaphysical Campigli and de Chirico; and the restless, expressionist Informels all packed into small salons decked with suitably avant-garde furnishings. (☑02 2024 0568; www.fondazioneboschidistefano.it; Via Giorgio Jan 15; admission free; ⊗9am-7.30pm Tue-Sun; MLima)

Galleria d'Arte Moderna
GALLERY

3 ⊙ Map p44, B3

Napoleon's temporary Milanese home, the 18th-century Villa Reale, now houses Milan's modern-art collection. Made up of bequests from leading Milanese families, the collection contains a wide-ranging spread of 19th- and 20th-century Italian and international art, progressing from pieces by neoclassical sculptor Canova (in the ballroom) to futurist painters Giacomo Balla and Umberto Boccioni. (GAM; ☑02 7600 2819; www.gam-milano.com; Via Palestro 16; adult/reduced €5/3; ⊗9am-5.30pm Tue-Sun; MPalestro)

Padiglione d'Arte Contemporanea
GALLERY

4 ⊙ Map p44, B3

Art and design intertwine at the city's ground-breaking contemporary galleries. Leading the pack is PAC, which mounts experimental exhibitions in photography, multimedia and contemporary art. (PAC; ☑02 8844 6359; www.pacmilano.it; Via Palestro 14; adult/reduced €8/6.50; ⊗9.30am-7.30pm Tue, Wed & Fri-Sun, to 10.30pm Thu; MPalestro)

Eating

Bagutta
MILANESE €€€

5 ✖ Map p44, B4

The Ministry of Cultural Resources calls Bagutta a historical landmark, but your taste buds will call it fabulous:

Top Tip

'House Museum' Card

The **Case Museo card** (adult/reduced €15/10; www.casemuseomilano.it) gives discounted access to Milan's four historic house museums: Museo Bagatti Valsecchi (p43), the Piero Portaluppi–designed **Villa Necchi Campiglio** (Map p44, C4; Via Mozart 14; ⏰10am-6pm Wed-Sun), the Casa Museo Boschi-di Stefano (p45) and the 19th-century Museo Poldi Pezzoli (p40). Valid for six months, it also entitles the bearer to a 10% discount in the museums' bookshops. You can purchase the card at any of the house museums.

the tasty lamb chops with sage and the melt-away spinach gnocchi with gorgonzola have kept napkins expectantly tucked under chins here since 1920. (☎02 7600 2767; www.bagutta.it; Via Bagutta 14; meals €40-50; ⏰12.30-10.30pm Mon-Sat; Ⓜ San Babila)

Corsia del Giardino   MODERN ITALIAN €€

Named for the gardens that once lined Via Manzoni, this contemporary cafe-cum-restaurant occupies a leafy niche off the main drag (see 28 Ⓐ Map p44, A4). Its sleek interior and elegant menu match the stylish clientele, workers from nearby shops in the Quad, who come here for top-quality salads, meat plates with 18-month aged Parma ham, artisanal ice cream and sweet fruit tarts. (☎02 7628 0726; www.corsiadelgiardino.it; Via Manzoni 16; meals €20-30; ⏰8am-8.30pm Mon-Sat, from 9am Sun; Ⓜ Montenapoleone)

Gelato Giusto   GELATERIA €

6 🍴 Map p44, D1

This gelateria is a temple to Lombardy's luxurious milk products: everything here is 100% natural, handmade and locally sourced. What's more, owner Vittoria is a Maître Chocolatier constantly in search of innovative and delightful flavours such as pistachio, cinnamon and black currant, and ricotta with bitter orange. (☎02 2951 0284; http://gelatogiusto.it; Via San Gregorio 17; 2/4 scoops €2.50/4.50; ⏰noon-11pm Tue-Sat, to 9pm Sun; ♿; Ⓜ Porta Venezia)

Joia   ITALIAN €€€

7 🍴 Map p44, C1

Known for seasonal produce and light, clean flavours, the menu at Joia is imbued with poetry (a winter dish of globe and Jerusalem artichokes with sweet black salsify and pomegranate is entitled 'Beneath a snowy white carpet'). After the meat-heavy Milanese menu, Michelin-starred Pietro Leeman's green realm is nothing short of delightful. The €40 lunch deal is great value. (☎02 2952 2124; www.joia.it; Via Panfilo Castaldi 18; tasting menu €80; ⏰12.30-2.30pm & 7.30-11pm Mon-Fri, 7.30pm-midnight Sat; ❄🖊; Ⓜ Porta Venezia)

Al Bufera
TAPAS €€

 8 Map p44, D1

A rare treat in Milan is this gourmet tapas bar pioneered by Alice and Matheus. Plates of *piquillo* peppers stuffed with salt cod, garlicky Galician prawns and *pata negra* ham make a welcome alternative to typical *aperitivo* plates of carb-heavy focaccia and pasta. Larger dishes of paella and *fideua* (a typical type of Spanish pasta) are also available, both with shrimp and lobster. (☏ 02 3668 6993; www.albufera.it; Via Lecco 15; tapas €1.50-10, paella €16-35; Ⓜ Porta Venezia)

Pavé
PASTRIES

 9 Map p44, C1

Try not to argue over the *frolla al cacao,* an insanely good crumb tart filled with a sinfully good ganache and topped by raw chocolate nuggets. After all, it's just one of the temptations dreamed up by pastry maestros Diego, Luca and Giovanni. There's also San Franciscan sourdough, savoury brioche filled with ricotta and sundried tomatoes, and almond kipfel. (☏ 02 9439 2259; www.pavemilano.com; Via Felice Casati 27; pastries €1.50-5.50, salads €6.50; ⏱ 8am-8pm Tue-Fri, 8.30am-7pm Sat & Sun; 🖋; Ⓜ Porta Venezia)

Chic & Go
SANDWICHES €

 10 Map p44, A4

Only in the Quad: stylish fast food such as lobster *panini*, velouté of asparagus and saffron-scented bulgur salads. As you'd expect, there's only bespoke tailoring here: choose a bread of your liking (sesame, poppy seed, bagel or baguette) then add first-class toppings such as Angus beef tartare, crabmeat mixed with paprika-spiced mayonnaise, and *mortadella* (pork cold cut) from Prato. De-licious. (☏ 02 78 26 48; www.chic-and-go.com; Via Bigli 20; sandwiches €5-14; 🖋; Ⓜ Montenapoleone)

Understand
The Milanese Larder

The food of Milan may not be redolent of the sun, but its quintessential dishes are still richly golden-hued. *Cotoletta* (sliced buttery veal with a burnished breadcrumb crust) and mellow yellow risotto Milanese (Po Valley carnaroli rice enriched with bone marrow and tinted with saffron) are cases in point. Other gold standards include osso buco, a veal-shank stew scattered with *gremolata* (parsley, garlic and lemon-rind); the polenta that accompanies meat or mushroom dishes; pumpkin-stuffed sage-scented ravioli; *panettone,* the eggy, briochelike Christmas bread; *mostarda di frutta,* Cremona's mustard-laced sweet preserves and Lombardy's rich bounty of cheese.

Lon Fon
CHINESE €€

11 Map p44, C1

Packed with pundits, this Cantonese restaurant is run by a mother-and-daughter team, Rita and Pui. You can count on veal and onion dumplings, whole crabs, and steamed fish with ginger and spring vegetables. They're happy to improvise with seasonal ingredients, such as artichokes, as well. (☏02 2940 5153; Via Lazzaretto 10; mains €30-45; ☻noon-3pm & 7-11.30pm; ❄; Ⓜ Repubblica)

Warsa
AFRICAN €€

12 Map p44, D2

Warm, elegant and atmospheric, Warsa serves authentic curries – lentil, beef or fish – Eritrean-style atop *injera* (flat bread). Eating is done with your hands. There's also a selection of South African wine. (☏02 20 16 73; www.ristorantewarsa. it; Via Melzo 16; meals €25; ☻noon-3pm & 7-11.30pm Thu-Tue; Ⓜ Porta Venezia)

Drinking

Nottingham Forest
COCKTAIL BAR

13 Map p44, D4

If Michelin awarded stars for bars, Nottingham Forest would have a clutch of them. This eclectically decorated Asian-cum-African tiki bar named after an English football team is the outpost of molecular mixologist Dario Comino, who conjures smoking cocktails packed with dry ice and ingenuity. Unique cocktails include the

Elite, a mix of vodka, ground pearls and sake – supposedly an aphrodisiac. (www.nottingham-forest.com; Viale Piave 1; cocktails €10; ☻6.30pm-2am Tue-Sat, 6pm-1am Sun; ☐9, 23)

Pandenus
BAR

14 Map p44, C1

Originally a bakery, Pandenus was named after the walnut bread that used to emerge from its (still active) oven. Now the focaccia, *pizzetta* and bruschetta on its burgeoning *aperitivo* bar are some of the best in town. Given its proximity to the Marconi Foundation (which is dedicated to contemporary art), expect a good-looking, arty crowd. (☏02 2952 8018; www.pandenus.it; Via Tadino 15; cocktails €8; brunch €20; ☻noon-1am; ☎; Ⓜ Porta Venezia)

HClub Diana
COCKTAIL BAR

15 Map p44, D2

Secreted behind a vast leather curtain at the back of the Sheraton, *aperitivo* at HClub Diana is one of Milan's most varied. Grab a freshly crushed peach bellini and lounge with the fashion pack around the low-lit garden pool in the shade of magnolia trees. (☏02 2058 2081; www.sheraton.com/dianamajestic; Viale Piave 42, Sheraton Diana Majestic; cocktails €10, brunch €33; ☻7am-1am; ☎; Ⓜ Porta Venezia)

Vinile
WINE BAR

16 Map p44, C1

Calling all comic connoisseurs and geeks, Vinile serves a limited-

Bar Basso

production wine list, Italian craft beers, and artisanal cold cuts and crostini in the midst of an impressive collection of *Star Wars* and Marvel memorabilia. Check out its Facebook page for community art and music events. (📞02 3651 4233; Via Tadino 17; drinks €4-6; brunch €18; 🕙11am-11.30pm Tue-Sun; Ⓜ Porta Venezia)

La Belle Aurore
BAR

17 🍷 Map p44, E3

A local favourite, this old-style bar recalls the city of Buenos Aires. It attracts a laid-back, diverse crowd from breakfast through to *aperitivo* to late-night, wine-soaked chats. (📞02

2940 6212; Via P G Abamonti 1; 🕙7-2am Mon-Sat; 🚍5, 23)

Bar Basso
BAR

18 🍷 Map p44, E2

This elegant corner bar is home of the *sbagliato,* a negroni made with *prosecco* instead of gin, as well as the brilliant concept of *mangia e bevi* (eat and drink), involving a super-sized goblet of strawberries, cream and *nocciola* (hazelnut) ice cream and a large slug of some kind of booze. (📞02 2940 0580; http://barbasso.com; Via Plinio 39; cocktails €7; 🕙9-1.15am Wed-Mon; Ⓜ Lima)

Local Life

Art Nouveau Architecture

The Allied bombs of WWII wreaked a terrible toll on Milan, but dotted among the postwar workarounds is some of the finest fin de siècle Liberty architecture in Italy. The best can be found around Porta Venezia. Treasures include **Casa Guazzoni** (Via Malpighi 12; M Porta Venezia), with its intricate wrought-iron balconies; **Casa Galimberti** (Via Malpighi 3; M Porta Venezia), with its ceramic tiles depicting bourgeois beauties; and the former **Cinema Dumont** (Via Frisi 2; M Porta Venezia), with its concrete garlands of flowers.

Sant'Ambroeus

CAFE

19 Map p44, B4

This belle époque bar with its glittering Murano chandelier and counter full of sugary confectionary is something of an institution in the Quad. It is frequented by sharp-suited clients slugging espresso and expensive cocktails, and women of a certain age who come to take tea in the salon or pick up intricately decorated celebration cakes. (📞02 7600 0540; www.santambroeusmilano.it; Corso Matteotti 7; cocktails €10; ⏱7.45am-8.30pm; M San Babila)

Armani Privé

CLUB

20 Map p44, A3

In the basement of the Armani superstore, this club has a subtle Japanese–modernist aesthetic, the calm of which you'll need after the hysteria of getting in and clocking the drinks prices. Boobs, botox and blonde hair (or a dinner booking at Nobu) will help with the door police. (📞02 6231 2655; Via Gastone Pisoni 1; cocktails €20; ⏱11.30pm-3.30am Wed-Sat; M Montenapoleone)

Entertainment

Spazio Oberdan

CINEMA

21 ⭐ Map p44, C2

The riches of Milan's *cineteca* (cinematheque, or film library) are screened downstairs, while upstairs there's a program of exhibitions from stills to video art. The original cinema was redesigned by architect Gae Aulenti, better known for her work on Cadorna station and Paris' Musée d'Orsay. (📞02 7740 6316; www.cinetecamilano.it; Viale Vittorio Veneto 2; M Porta Venezia)

Shopping

Pellini

JEWELLERY, ACCESSORIES

22 Map p44, A3

For unique, one-off costume jewellery pieces, bags and hair pieces, look no further than the boutique of Donatella Pellini, granddaughter of famous costume designer Emma Pellini. The Pellini women have been making their trademark resin jewellery for three generations, and their fanciful creations incorporating flowers, sand

and fabric are surprisingly affordable. ([☎]02 7600 8084; www.pellini.it; Via Manzoni 20; [◷]3.30-7.30pm Mon, 9.30am-7.30pm Tue-Sat Sep-Jul; [M]Montenapoleone)

Mutinelli
ACCESSORIES

25 [🔒] Map p44, D2

Millayne bonnets were all the rage in the 15th and 16th centuries, so much so that they gave the city its name. Founded a few centuries later in 1888, Mutinelli is the oldest milliner in Milan, and its historic premises are filled to the rafters with stylish headgear made of the finest felt, fabric, leather and Ecuadorean toquilla palm.

Walking sticks, umbrellas and suspenders can also be purchased for a dapper finish. ([☎]02 669 19 71; www.mutinellicappellimilano.com; Corso Buenos Aires 5; [◷]3-7.30pm Mon, 10am-1pm & 3-7.30pm Tue-Sat; [M]Porta Venezia)

Atelier Bergnach
FASHION

24 [🔒] Map p44, D1

Elena Bergnach has been making skirts for Milanese women for more than 13 years. These aren't just any skirts, but skirts with real personality, made with brocade from India or silk from Como, and then cut into 20 different patterns and pleated, ruffled and slashed in asymmetrical shapes. Each skirt is then tweaked on-site to make sure it fits the customer perfectly. (www.atelierbergnach.com; Via Tadino 15; [◷]10am-1pm & 3-7.30pm Tue-Sat; [M]Porta Venezia)

Madina Milano
BEAUTY

25 [🔒] Map p44, B4

Madina is Milan's own cult cosmetics label. Complimentary makeovers let you experiment with the extraordinary range of colours and finishes. ([☎]02 7601 1692; www.madina.it; Corso Venezia 23; [◷]10am-7pm; [M]Cordusio)

Car Shoe
SHOES

26 [🔒] Map p44, B4

Now under the wing of Patrizio Bertelli (Mr Prada), the original '60s hybrid of sport shoe and smart-casual loafer is set for a comeback in this flagship shop. To counter the lothario

[🔍] Local Life
Fondazione Nicola Trussardi

Fashion house Trussardi's provocative, nonprofit **Fondazione Nicola Trussardi** ([☎]02 806 88 21; www.fondazionenicolatrussardi.com) is neither a museum nor a collection, but acts as an agency for the promotion of contemporary art within unusual historic or architectural venues. Through its work, the foundation has restored and reopened a number of historic buildings, such as Palazzo Litta and Palazzo Dugnani, where international artists have been invited to create new work for one-off events. Exhibits take place in venues all over the city; check the website for details.

Understand

Fashion City

Cobblers, seamstresses, tailors and milliners, Italy's artisans have been shoeing, dressing and adorning Europe's affluent classes with the finest fashion money can buy since the 11th century.

The Renaissance

As the Renaissance shone its light on art, music and literature, so fashion flourished, promoted by the celebrities of the day, the Florentine Medicis. Ostentatious fashion dictated status and wealth: hats, snoods, cauls and other headdresses were swagged, draped and jewelled; gowns had sweeping floor-length sleeves and were made of fine linens, silks, brocades and lace. Styles were borrowed, adapted and disseminated throughout Italy and beyond. In France, the high-heeled shoe was adopted after Catherine de Medici became Queen of France in 1547.

From Florence to Milan

Although the origins of the Italian fashion scene were in Florence, the rigidly controlled salons stifled creativity and forced designers to look elsewhere. Breaking with tradition, Walter Albini held his first show in Milan in 1971. Away from the fashion establishment, he was able to experiment, producing the first ready-to-wear collection and enhancing the role of the designer as the creative force behind the brand. It was a resounding success and from then on Milan began to eclipse Florence as the fashion capital of Italy.

Fashion Capital

Milan's rise to global fashion mecca was far from random. First, thanks to its geographic position, the city had historically strong links with European markets. It was also Italy's capital of finance, advertising, TV and publishing, with both *Vogue* and *Amica* magazines based in the city. What's more, Milan had always had a clothing industry based around the historic textile and silk production of upper Lombardy. And, with the city's particular postwar focus on trade fairs, it provided a natural marketplace for the exchange of goods, ideas and information. As a result, by the 1980s a new generation of designers – Armani, Versace, Prada, Ferragamo and Dolce & Gabbana – emerged to conquer the world, transforming shoes, bags, fragrances and sunglasses into the new badges of status and wealth.

reputation, it now also does ranges for women and kids. (☏ 02 7602 4027; www.carshoe.com; Via della Spiga 1; ⏰ 10am-7.30pm Mon-Sat, 11am-7pm Sun; Ⓜ San Babila)

Sermoneta ACCESSORIES

27 Map p44, B3

A hole in the wall on chic Via della Spiga, Sermoneta's boutique store sells standards such as hand-stitched calfskin gloves alongside more unique styles made of pony skin or peccary hide. (☏ 02 7631 8903; www. sermonetagloves.com; Via della Spiga 46; ⏰ 10am-7pm Mon-Sat, from 11am Sun; Ⓜ Montenapoleone)

Gallo ACCESSORIES

28 Map p44, A4

Gallo may spice up its seasonal collections but it's the perennial striped knee socks that locals love for adding secret colour to drab business attire. The range for men, women, children and babes is equally wide. You'll never risk losing these beauties in the dryer, and you won't want to at €12 to €35 a pop. (☏ 02 78 36 02; www.gallospa.it; Via Manzoni 16; ⏰ 10am-7pm; Ⓜ Montenapoleone)

Doriani FASHION, ACCESSORIES

29 Map p44, B4

Established in 1930, Doriani is renowned for its ultrasoft cashmere knits, including polo shirts, cardigans and sweaters. Its quintessentially understated menswear is sought after by politicians, footballers and businessmen who prize the classic shapes and subtle, subdued colour palette. (☏ 02 7602 1527; www.doriani.it; Via Sant'Andrea 7; ⏰ 10am-7.30pm Tue-Sun; Ⓜ Montenapoleone)

DMagazine FASHION

30 Map p44, A3

Given you usually have to schlep out of town for deeply discounted designer threads, what's up with this perversely central outlet? Yes, all the major labels are here, but tend to be the stranger of their kind. However, if you dig deep, you can unearth designer finds for as little as 20% of the original retail price. (☏ 02 7600 6027; www.dmagazine.it; Via Manzoni 44; ⏰ 10am-7.30pm; Ⓜ Montenapoleone)

Explore

Brera & Parco Sempione

Brera's tight cobbled streets and ancient buildings are a reminder that Milan wasn't always a modern metropolis. At the heart of the neighbourhood is the 17th-century Accademia di Belle Arti, the city's famous art school. Around it are galleries, some of the city's most fashionable restaurants and lively bars. To the west the grand Castello Sforzesco bookends the city's largest public park, Parco Sempione.

The Sights in a Day

☼ Spend the morning browsing Napoleon's superbly curated collection of Old Masters at the **Pinacoteca di Brera** (p58). The artworks are displayed in schools of style according to the original intention of the gallery, which was meant to complement courses at the academy (downstairs from the Pinacoteca). When you hit art overload, a midmorning drink might be in order at the student bar downstairs or up the road at **N'Ombra de Vin** (p66).

☼ For lunch, wander Brera's warren of streets in search of some of its excellent restaurants: try sophisticated French-influenced cooking at **Fioraio Bianchi** (p65) or hearty Roman fare at **Volemose Bene** (p64). Afterwards go west to **Castello Sforzesco** (p56) to walk the battlements, or explore Milan's history of design at the **Triennale di Milano** (p63).

☾ Early evening warrants a walk in the park up to Napoleon's magnificent triumphal arch, the **Arco della Pace** (p63). It's conveniently surrounded by excellent *aperitivo* (see p97) bars, which are always packed out. For something more sophisticated, head to **Dry** (p66) or the **Bulgari Hotel** (p68), where you can while away the evening in a tranquil garden.

◉ Top Sights

Castello Sforzesco (p56)

Pinacoteca di Brera (p58)

♥ Best of Milan

Art

Pinacoteca di Brera (p58)

Design

Triennale di Milano (p63)

Studio Museo Achille Castiglioni (p63)

Eating

Volemose Bene (p64)

Pescheria da Claudio (p65)

Ristorante Solferino (p65)

Drinking

Bulgari Hotel (p68)

N'Ombra de Vin (p66)

Dry (p66)

Getting There

Ⓜ **Metro** For the Pinacoteca, use Montenapoleone on M3 (yellow line) and Lanza on M2 (green line).

Ⓜ **Metro** For the castle and park, use Cairoli on M1 (red line) or Lanza on M2 (green line).

🚋 **Tram** Number 1 gives good access to shopping street Via Vetero.

Top Sights
Castello Sforzesco

Originally a Visconti fortress, this iconic red-brick castle was later home to the mighty Sforza dynasty who ruled Renaissance Milan. The castle's defences were designed by the multitalented Leonardo da Vinci; Napoleon later drained the moat and removed the drawbridges. Today it shelters seven specialised museums that gather together intriguing fragments of Milan's cultural and civic history, from the medieval equestrian tomb of Bernabò Visconti to Michelangelo's *Rondanini Pietà*, his final unfinished masterpiece.

👁 Map p62, B4

www.milanocastello.it

Piazza Castello

adult/reduced €5/3

🕓9am-7.30pm Tue-Sun, to 10.30pm Thu

Ⓜ Cairoli

Castello Sforzesco tower

Don't Miss

The Architecture

To withstand any challenges to their power, Milan's politicking Sforzas gave the castle its robust medieval layout. Francesco invited Florentine architect Filarete to design the high central tower in 1452 to soften the appearance and affect an elegant residence rather than a barracks. Thick round towers, faced with diamond-shaped *serizzo* granite, bolstered the ramparts, and Galeazzo Maria later embellished the Rocchetta and the Ducal Courtyard with Renaissance porticos. Inside, the ducal apartments were endowed with pavilion vaults and later decorated by Leonardo da Vinci himself, under the patronage of Ludovico Sforza (1452–1508).

Civiche Raccolta d'Arte Antica

Housed in the ducal apartments, the Museum of Ancient Art has a stellar collection. From paleo-Christian frescoes to the fine equestrian tomb of Bernarbò Visconti and sculpted reliefs depicting Milan's triumph over Barbarossa, the artworks relate the birth of Italy's first city *comune*. Da Vinci had a hand in the interior decor, which sports coats of arms, murals and the Gonfalcon of the King of Spain who married here in 1555.

Rondanini Pietà

Named for the Roman palace where it long stood, Michelangelo's *Rondanini Pietà* is his final, and some say finest, piece of work. Depicting a slender Mary struggling to support the dying figure of Christ, the sculpture conveys an aching spirituality through its exaggerated simplicity, leading many to consider it the earliest piece of modern art. It now stands resplendent among the frescoes of the castle's 16th-century Spanish Hospital.

☑ Top Tips

- Admission to the castle museums is free every Tuesday from 2pm.
- To tour the castle's battlements and underground rooms, consider a tour with **Ad Artem**. (☎02 659 77 28; http://adartem.it; Via Melchiorre Gioia 1; tours €8-17.50; ⏲9am-1pm & 2-4pm; 👪; Ⓜ Sondrio)
- If you're short on time, the best collection is the Civiche Raccolte d'Arte Antica (Museum of Ancient Art), and Michelangelo's *Rondanini* is unmissable.

✕ Take a Break

If the weather's nice, have a picnic in the park or a drink on the terrace of Bar Bianco (p67).

For something more substantial, consider a plate of *crudo* (raw seafood) at Pescheria da Claudio (p65); or, in the evening, stroll across the park for *aperitivo* at Living (p64).

Top Sights
Pinacoteca di Brera

Located upstairs from the Brera Academy (still one of Italy's most prestigious art schools), this gallery houses Milan's impressive collection of Old Masters, much of it 'lifted' from Venice by Napoleon. Rembrandt, Goya and Van Dyck all have a place in the collection, but you're here to see the Italians: Titian, Tintoretto, Veronese and the Bellini brothers. Much of the work has tremendous emotional clout, most notably Mantegna's brutal *Cristo morto nel Sepolcro e tre Dolenti* (Lamentation over the Dead Christ).

👁 Map p62, D3

📞 02 7226 3264

www.brera.beniculturali.it

Via Brera 28

adult/reduced €10/7

🕑 8.30am-7.15pm Tue-Sun

Ⓜ Lanza, Montenapoleone

Sala XXXVI, Pinacoteca di Brera

Don't Miss

Lombard Frescoes

The Brera collection starts with a blast of Renaissance brilliance, launching you down a corridor lined with Donato Bramante's *Men at Arms* and Bernardino Luini's frescoes from the suppressed church of La Pace and Casa Pelucca. While Luini's tableau of girls playing 'hot-cockles' illustrates the influence of Leonardo da Vinci in its blending of Renaissance innovations with indigenous Milanese scenes, Bramante's soldiers, meant for the Barons' Hall at Casa Visconti, define a new understanding of illusionistic perspective. Viewed from below, the figures loom upwards, their gigantic forms emerging from architectural frames.

Oratorio di Mocchirolo

To the left side of the entrance hall in Room IA is a reconstruction of the oratory of Mocchirolo and its splendid fresco cycle, thought to be the work of Giotto. Particularly notable is the *Crucifixion*, which displays Giotto's typically strong sense of visual narrative and expressive realism.

Bellini & Mantegna

The works of Giovanni Bellini and Andrea Mantegna, displayed in room VI, are some of the highlights of the Pinacoteca's Venetians. Like Bramante before him, Mantegna had a passion for rigorous perspective and a love of classicism that combined to create the stunningly unsentimental *Cristo morto nel Sepolcro e tre Dolenti*, with its violent foreshortening of Christ's corpse. Although influenced by Mantegna, Bellini's sad-eyed Madonnas and exquisitely tender *Pietà* demonstrate the progressing humanisation of the subject, enhanced by the expressive effects of colour and light in the landscape around them.

☑ Top Tips

▶ You'll need at least half a day to cover the gallery's 38 rooms at a reasonable pace.

▶ The gallery is upstairs on the 1st floor. Stairs are behind Canova's bronze statue of Napoleon posing as a demigod in the courtyard.

▶ Audio guides are available in Italian, French, English, Spanish and German for €5.

▶ Don't miss the glass-walled restoration laboratory, where you can see conservators at work.

✕ Take a Break

The Pinacoteca's treasures can be overwhelming, so head downstairs and join students for a post-life-drawing-class Peroni.

For a light lunch amid flowers head to French-inspired Fioraio Bianchi (p65), or continue north to Zazà Ramen (p65) for superior bowls of noodles.

Titian, Tintoretto & Veronese

The high-water mark of the Renaissance dawned in Venice in the 16th century with an extraordinary confluence of talent in the persons of Tizian Vercelli (Titian), Jacopo Tintoretto and Paolo Veronese. While Rome was in decline and the rest of Italy oppressed by moral mores that the licentious Venetians scoffed at, Venice had both the deep pockets of the doge and his stabilising iron rule. So wealth, patronage and art flourished, with Titian as protagonist. Room IX brings together some of their greatest works, including Titian's *St Jerome* and Veronese's *Cena in Casa di Simone* (Supper in the House of Simon).

The Jesi Collection: 20th Century

Located off room VIII is the Jesi Collection, donated in 1984. It includes the 12 sculptures and 68 paintings of Emilio Jesi, acquired in the 1930s, '40s and '50s. A welcome relief from the main gallery's religious pieces, these vibrant futurist canvases include Boccioni's fabulous *Rissa in Galleria* (Riot in the Gallery) and Carlo Carrà's *La Musa Metafisica* (Metaphysical Muse).

The Urbino School

One of the greatest painters of the early Renaissance, Piero della Francesca was engaged by Urbino's Count of Montefeltro in 1474. Although the Tuscan artist and mathematician is

PINACOTECA DI BRERA

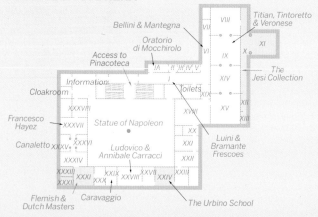

more famous for his cycle of frescoes in Arezzo's Basilica di San Francesco, the Montefeltro altarpiece, otherwise known as the *Brera Madonna* (1472–74), is the prize of room XXIV. As a counterpoint, take a look at Raphael's much looser and more natural *Wedding of the Virgin*, which was painted in 1504.

Caravaggio

Filled with the darkening palette and glimmering colours of the baroque Emilian school of the late 16th and early 17th century, room XXIX delivers an unexpected emotional thump. Home to the academy's only Caravaggio, *Cena in Emmaus* (Supper at Emmaus), the room is dark and brooding. Gone is the neat classicism of Raphael and the mannerist trickery of Carracci, and in its place is a potent naturalism, framed by an existential conflict between light and dark.

Flemish Masters

Amid its huge Italian collection, the academy inherited a small selection of Flemish and Dutch masters, now housed in rooms XXXI through to XXXIII. Rubens, Rembrandt and Van Dyck arrived from the Louvre in 1813, and in 1855 Peter Oggioni donated masters of the Antwerp school, such as Jan de Beer, along with German artists Herman Rode and Hans Memling. Seen in the context of all that has gone before, the cross-pollination from the Renaissance is particularly noticeable.

Il Bacio (The Kiss) by Francesco Hayez

The 19th Century

By the time you reach the final rooms and the early 19th century, at which time the gallery itself was emerging into prominence, the artwork becomes lighter, imbued with the romanticism and patriotism of a unified Italy. Breeze through Canaletto's atmospheric views of Venice to Francesco Hayez, pet portrait artist for the Lombard nobility and a director at the academy. His works include the intense and luminous *Il Bacio* (The Kiss; 1859), one of the most reproduced artworks in the gallery, which came to symbolize the hopes of the Risorgimento (reunification period).

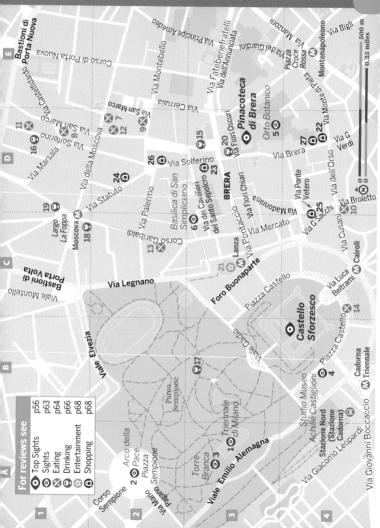

Bastioni di Porta Nuova
Via Castelfidardo
Corso di Porta Nuova
Via Principe Amedeo
Via Fatebenefratelli
Via dell'Annunciata
Via del Giardini
Via Manzoni
Via Bigli
Montenapoleone
Piazza Croce Rossa
Via Monte di Pietà
Via San Marco
Via San Marco
Via Montebello
Via Cernaia
Pinacoteca di Brera
Orto Botanico
500 m
0.25 miles
Via Solferino
Via Marsala
Via della Moscova
Via Fiori Oscuri
Via Brera
Via G Verdi
Via dell'Orso
Via Statuto
Via Palermo
Via Solferino
BRERA
Via Ponte Vetero
Largo La Foppa
Moscova
Basilica di San Simpliciano
Via dei Cavalleri del Santo Sepolcro
Via Fiori Chiari
Via Madonnina
Via Broletto
Via G Sacchi
Via Cusani
Via Mercato
Via Pontaccio
Corso Garibaldi
Lanza
Foro Buonaparte
Cairoli
Via Luca Beltrami
Via Legnano
Piazza Castello
Castello Sforzesco
Viale Montello
Bastioni di Porta Volta
Viale Elvezia
Parco Sempione
Piazza Castello
Piazza Castello
Viale Gadio
Cadorna Triennale
Cadorna
Stazione Nord (Stazione Cadorna)
Studio Museo Achille Castiglioni
Viale Emilio Alemagna
Triennale di Milano
Torre Branca
Arco della Pace
Piazza Sempione
Via Mario Pagano
Corso Sempione
Via Giacomo Leopardi
Via Giovanni Boccaccio

11
16
7
12
9
15
20
5
27
22
26
23
24
19
18
6
13
21
10
25
14
17
2
3
1
4

Sights

Triennale di Milano
MUSEUM

1 Map p62, A3

Italy's first Triennale took place in 1923 in Monza. It aimed to promote interest in Italian design and applied arts, from 'the spoon to the city', and its success led to the creation of Giovanni Muzio's **Palazzo d'Arte** in Milan in 1933. Since then this exhibition space has championed design in all its forms, although the triennale formula has since been replaced by long annual events, with international exhibits as part of the program. (02 72 43 41; www.triennaledesignmuseum. it; Viale Emilio Alemanga 6; adult/reduced €8/6.50; 10.30am-8.30pm Tue, Wed, Sat & Sun, to 11pm Thu & Fri; P M Cadorna)

Arco della Pace
LANDMARK

2 Map p62, A2

Situated at the northwestern edge of Parco Sempione is Napoleon's 25m-high triumphal arch. Designed by Luigi Cagnola in 1807, it echoes Paris' Arc de Triomphe and marks the start of Corso Sempione, the main road that connects Milan to Paris via the Simplon (Sempione) Pass. Ironically, thanks to Napoleon's fall in 1814, its neoclassical facade was finished in 1838 with bas-reliefs not of Napoleon's victories, as was intended, but with scenes from the Battle of Leipzig (1813), depicting his defeat. (Piazza Sempione; M Moscova, Cairoli)

Torre Branca
LANDMARK

3 Map p62, A3

Giò Ponti's spindly 1933 steel tower (built in two months flat for a Triennale exhibition) provides a fantastic 108m-high viewing platform over Parco Sempione. Take the lift up at sunset, or at night to watch the city lights twinkle, and lord it over the Cavalli Café crowd below. (02 331 41 20; admission €5; 3-7pm & 8.30pm-midnight Tue, Thu & Fri, 10.30am-12.30pm & 3pm-midnight Wed, 10.30am-2pm & 2.30pm-midnight Sat & Sun May-Sep, closes 6.30pm Oct-Apr; M Cadorna)

Studio Museo Achille Castiglioni
MUSEUM

4 Map p62, B4

Architect, designer and teacher Achille Castiglioni was one of Italy's most influential 20th-century thinkers. This is the studio where he worked daily until his death in 2002, and the hour-long tours vividly illuminate his intelligent but playful creative process. Details abound and await discovery: job folders printed with specially produced numerical stamps; scale models of his Hilly sofa designed for Cassina; and a host of inspirational objects from joke glasses to bicycle seats. (02 7243 4231; www.achillecastiglioni.it; Piazza Castello 27; adult/reduced €10/7; tours 10am, 11am & noon Tue-Fri, 6.30pm, 7.30pm & 8.30pm Thu; M Cadorna)

◯ Local Life

Parco Sempione

Parco Sempione (admission free; ☉6.30am–nightfall; Ⓜ Cadorna, Lanza) was once the preserve of hunting Sforza dukes, until Napoleon came to town and set about landscaping. First the French carved out orchards, then Napoleon added a mini-colosseum, the **Arena Civica**, and finally the idea for a public park was mooted in 1891. It was a resounding success, and today Milanese of all ages come to enjoy its winding paths and ornamental ponds. Bookending the park, opposite the Castello Sforzesco, is Napoleon's **Arco della Pace** (p63). It's ringed by popular bars such as **Living** (Map p62, A2; ☏ 02 3310 0824; www.livingmilano.com; Piazza Sempione 2; cocktails €8-10; ☉8am–2am; Ⓜ Moscova) and **Bhangrabar** (Map p62, A2; ☏ 02 3493 4469; www.bhangrabar. it; Corso Sempione 1; ☉6pm–2am; 🚊1, 19), making it a prime *aperitivo* spot.

Orto Botanico

GARDENS

 5 Map p62, D3

Maria Teresa had the towering gingko planted here in 1777, when she turned the former Jesuit vegetable patch into an open-air lecture hall for budding botanists (the wunderkind of the Enlightenment). This fragrant, walled garden is still filled with medicinal plants and is a pleasant place for a stroll. (www.

brera.unimi.it; Via Brera 28; admission free; ☉9am–noon & 2-5pm Mon-Fri, 10am-4pm Sat Sep, Oct & Feb-Jun, 9am–12.30pm Mon-Fri, 10am-4pm Sat Nov-Jan & Jul-Aug; Ⓜ Montenapoleone)

Basilica di San Simpliciano

CHURCH

6 Map p62, C3

San Simpliciano is one St Ambrose's four Milanese churches, built on a paleo-Christian cemetery with a red-brick Romanesque wrapping. Martyrs Sisinio, Martirio and Alessandro are buried here, and supposedly rose from their graves in the form of doves to give courage to the Lombard League in the battle of Legnano in 1176, leading to the defeat of Barbarossa. The beautiful fresco in the apse is Bergognone's *Coronation of the Virgin* (1515). (☏ 02 86 22 74; www.sansimpliciano. it; Piazza San Simpliciano 7; ☉9.30-11.30am & 3-6pm; Ⓜ Lanza)

Eating

Volemose Bene

OSTERIA €€

7 Map p62, D2

Deliberately kitsch rustic Roman interiors (checked tablecloths, strings of garlic, straw flagons), a loud crush of diners and stunningly good Roman cooking are the ingredients of this restaurant, which lives up to its name (roughly translated as 'caring for each other'). Don't miss Jewish-style artichokes, roast lamb with potatoes or fiery *pasta all'amatriciana* (pasta with spicy tomato sauce, *pecorino* cheese and bacon). (📞02 3655 9618; www.volemosebenemilano.it; Via della Moscova 25; meals €30; 🕐noon-2.30pm & 7.30-11.30pm; Ⓜ Moscova)

Ristorante Solferino
MILANESE €€€

8 Map p62, D1

Salivary glands have worked overtime here for a century, thanks to hearty classics such as osso buco swathed in risotto, unexpected delights such as fish tortelloni, and an extensive vegetarian menu. Join Italian film stars risking their figures with the in-house pastry chef's creations, and journalists steadily losing their objectivity over a superior wine selection. (📞02 2900 5748; www.ilsolferino.com; Via Castelfidardo 2; meals €45-60; 🕐noon-2.30pm & 6-11.30pm; ❄🥢; Ⓜ Moscova)

Fioraio Bianchi Caffè
ITALIAN, FRENCH €€€

9 Map p62, D2

This former florist's shop is great for a light French-influenced lunch, or an excellent *aperitivo* among the flowers. Dinners are fresh and inventive with particularly delicious border-crossing desserts, from Provencal lavender brûlée to an Arab-inflected cassata cup. (📞02 2901 4390; www.fioraiobianchicaffe.it; Via Montebello 7; meals €45-60; 🕐12.30-2.30pm & 8.30-11pm Mon-Sat; Ⓜ Moscova)

Pescheria da Claudio
SEAFOOD €€

10 Map p62, D4

Join the savvy suits for a power lunch or early dinner of *pesce crudo* (raw fish). Plates of marinated tuna, mixed salmon, tuna and white fish with pistachios, or lightly blanched octopus carpaccio are consumed with a glass of light fizz. Order and pay at the cashier, then collect your lunch from the servers. (📞02 8691 5741; www.pescheriadaclaudio.it; Via Cusani 1; meals €35-55; 🕐12.30-2.30pm & 7.30-10.30pm Tue-Sat; ❄; Ⓜ Cairoli)

Zazà Ramen
ASIAN €€

11 Map p62, D1

Owned by a Dutch chef and a Japanese entrepreneur, this noodle bar offers a range of seasonal ramen dishes with Italo-Asian condiments as well as appetisers such as asparagus with toasted-sesame-seed dressing. It also does an unusual twist on a *spritz* (a type of cocktail made with prosecco), substituting the Campari bitter for umeshu, a Japanese plum distillate. (📞02 3679 9000; http://zazaramen.it; Via Solferino 48; meals €30; 🕐noon-3pm & 7pm-midnight Mon & Wed-Sun; 🥢; Ⓜ Moscova)

Latteria di San Marco
TRATTORIA €€

12 Map p62, D2

If you can snare a seat in this tiny and ever-popular restaurant, you'll find old favourites such as *maccheroni al pomodoro e burro* (pasta with tomatoes and butter) mixed in with chef Arturo's own creations, such as his lemony meatballs or *riso al salto* (risotto fritters), on the daily-changing menu. (☑02 659 76 53; Via San Marco 24; meals €35-40; ☺12.30-2.30pm & 7.30-10pm Mon-Fri; Ⓜ Moscova)

Le Rosse
ITALIAN €

14 Map p62, C2

Simple platters of superior cold cuts, carpaccio, quiches and Lombard cheeses accompany glasses of interesting small-production wines at this laid-back wine bar with outdoor seating on Corso Garibaldi. The wild-boar salami from the Nebrodi mountains in Sicily is excellent, as is the Alpine cheese board. (☑02 9287 0416; www.lerosse.it; Corso Garibaldi 79; meals €25;

Q Local Life
Milanese Sushi

Italians love their *crudo* (raw seafood), almost as much as the Japanese. *Crudo's* appeal draws on the same taste and texture elements as sushi – a deceptively simple balance of fat, salt and acid – but uses olive oil, vinegar or citrus, sea salt and pepper instead of soy, pickle and wasabi. The Milanese can't get enough, either Italian-style, trad Japanese or a fusion of the two, and strangely often refer to all forms of *crudo* as 'sushi'. For fabulously fresh and simple fish, try local Da Claudio (p65) and for smart sushi and sashimi head to Navigli for Basara (p95).

☺12.30-3pm & 6.30pm-midnight Mon-Sat; Ⓜ Lanza, Moscova)

Al Politico
SANDWICHES €

14 Map p62, C4

This sandwich kiosk crammed with locals gives you an idea of Milan's sharp sense of humour. All the handsomely stuffed sandwiches are named after politicians, requiring diners to struggle between matching their political allegiances with their favourite stuffing. Table seating surrounds the kiosk. (Piazza Castello 5; sandwiches €5-8; ☺8am-8pm; Ⓜ Cairoli, Cadorna)

Drinking

N'Ombra de Vin
WINE BAR

15 Ⓣ Map p62, D3

This *enoteca* (wine bar) is set in a one-time Augustine refectory. Tastings can be had all day and you can also indulge in food such as *carpaccio di pesce spade agli agrumi* (swordfish carpaccio prepared with citrus) from a limited menu. Check the website for occasional cultural events and DJ nights. (☑02 659 96 50; www.nombradevin.it; Via San Marco 2; ☺10-2am; Ⓜ Lanza, Moscova)

Dry
COCKTAIL BAR

16 Ⓣ Map p62, D1

The brainchild of Michelin-starred chef Andrea Berton, Dry mixes its cocktails with gourmet pizzas.

Sushi

The inventive cocktail list includes the Corpse Reviver (London Dry gin, cointreau, Cocchi Americano and lemon juice) and the Martinez (Boompjes genever, vermouth, Maraschino liqueur and Boker's bitters), the latter inspired by French gold hunters in Martinez, the birthplace of barman Jerry Thomas. (☑02 6379 3414; www.drymilano.it; Via Solferino 33; cocktails €8-13, meals €20-25; ⊙7pm-midnight; MMoscova)

Bar Bianco
BAR

17 Ⓟ Map p62, B3

Ricardo Griffini's Bar Bianco was built as a milk bar for the Tenth Triennale (1954). Still popular with mums and

toddlers in the daytime and a hip *aperitivo* crowd come evening, it's the best bar in Parco Sempione. The patio seats are good for people-watching, but aim for the upper terrace – it's like having a cocktail in a treehouse. (☑02 8699 2026; www.bar-bianco.com; Parco Sempione; ⊙10-1am Mon-Thu & Sun, to 2am Fri & Sat May-Sep, 10am-6pm Oct-Apr; ☞; MLanza)

Bottiglieria Moscatelli
BAR

18 Ⓟ Map p62, C1

It may have been open since the Franco-Austrian war, but the decor at this popular bar belongs firmly in the 1950s. It's all about the wine here;

Local Life
Bulgari Hotel

Inside beneath the giant botanical sculptures or outside on the terrace, the *aperitivo* (see p97) scene at **Bulgari Hotel** (Map p62, D4; ☑02 805 80 51; www.bulgarihotel.com; Via Privata Fratelli Gabba 7b; �a7.30am-1am; MMontenapoleone) is an intense slice of Milanese life. Its private walled garden is a lovely place to sit any time of the day, but the early-evening cocktail hour is when the *bel mondo* (high society) descend. The second-cheapest wine on the list weighs in at €20 but it's cheap for the theatre, darling, and made more palatable by the endless stream of gourmet snacks sent forth by Neapolitan chef Roberto di Pinto.

perhaps have a glass with a plate of *coppa* (cured pork neck) and some bread. (☑02 655 46 02; Corso Garibaldi 93; aperitivo €8; �a7am-2am Mon-Sat, 9am-10pm Sun; MMoscova)

Radetzky Cafe   BAR
19 🍷 Map p62, D1

Fabulous banquette and window seating make Radetzky one of the most popular *aperitivo* places on this stylish, pedestrianised strip. Sunday brunch is also served. (☑02 657 26 45; Corso Garibaldi 105; �a8pm-1.30am Mon-Wed, to 2am Thu-Sat, 10-1.30am Sun; MMoscova)

Bar Jamaica   BAR
20 🍷 Map p62, D3

Bar Jamaica may no longer be the bohemian dive that gave Milan a fleeting reputation for brains as well as style, but it's still an unpretentious watering hole. Students from nearby Accademia di Brera nurse drinks on coveted pavement seats. (☑02 87 67 23; www.jamaicabar.it; Via Brera 32; cocktails €8, meals €25-35; �a9-2am; MLanza)

Entertainment

Piccolo Teatro Strehler   THEATRE
21 ⭐ Map p62, C3

This trailblazing theatre with seating for 960 people was designed by Marco Zanuso to address the size constraints of the original Piccolo Teatro. It has since gone on to become one of Milan's cultural powerhouses, and includes the Teatro Studio at Via Rivoli 6. (☑02 4241 1889; www.piccoloteatro.org; Largo Greppi; MLanza)

Shopping

Cavalli e Nastri   FASHION
22 🔒 Map p62, D4

This gorgeously colourful shop is known for its vintage clothes and accessories. It specialises in lovingly curated frocks, bags, jewellery and even shoes, sourced from early- and mid-20th-century Italian fashion houses, and priced accordingly. You'll find its **menswear store** (www.cavallienastri.com; Via Mora 3; ⏱10.30am-7.30pm Tue-Sun; 🚊2, 14) at Via Mora 3. (☑02 7200 0449; www.cavallienastri.com; Via Brera 2; ⏱10.30am-7.30pm Tue-Sat, 3.30-7.30pm Mon; Ⓜ Montenapoleone)

Malìparmi
FASHION

23 🔒 Map p62, D3

It all began in Padua with Marol Paresi combining her love of travel and her craft skills to create ethnically inspired and artfully beaded, embroidered and printed bags, sandals, jewellery and clothes. Now, with her daughter beside her, she has shops around the world, but her most colourful creations are still to be found here, close to home. (☑02 7209 3899; www.maliparmi.it; Via Solferino 3; ⏱3-7pm Mon, 10am-7pm Tue-Sat)

La Vetrina di Beryl
SHOES

24 🔒 Map p62, D2

Barbara Beryl's name was known to cultists around the world way before 'Manolo' became a byword for female desire. Stumbling upon this deceptively nondescript shop is like chancing upon the shoe racks at a *Vogue Italia* photo shoot. (☑02 65 42 78; Via Statuto 4; ⏱3.30-7.30pm Mon, 10.30am-2.30pm & 3.30-7.30pm Tue-Sat; Ⓜ Moscova)

Fabriano
ACCESSORIES, GIFTS

25 🔒 Map p62, D4

Stationery-tragics won't be the only ones going quietly gaga over Fabriano's goods. Everything from plain notebooks to linen pencil cases to kooky leather keyrings are exquisitely crafted. An ever-present sense of wit makes all the good taste even more attractive. The staff is delightful and wraps gifts with trademark flair. (☑02 7631 8754; www.fabrianoboutique.com; Via Ponte Vetero 17; ⏱1-7.30pm Mon, 10am-7.30pm Tue-Sat; Ⓜ Cairoli, 🚊1)

Kristina Ti
FASHION

26 🔒 Map p62, D2

Kristina Ti specialises in things that are swoon-inducingly pretty but never one-dimensionally girly. Slips and lingerie can be nicely boxed as gifts. (☑02 65 33 79; www.kristinati.com; Via Solferino 18; ⏱10am-7pm Tue-Sat, 3-7pm Mon; Ⓜ Moscova)

Rigadritto
GIFTS

27 🔒 Map p62, D4

Loads of little stickers, clips, pencils and decorated stationery fill this graphic, colourful space. Cat and dog T-shirts that turn humans into pets are delightful. (☑02 8058 2936; www.rigadritto.com; Via Brera 6; ⏱10.30am-7.30pm; Ⓜ Montenapoleone)

Explore

Porta Garibaldi & Isola

Home to César Pelli's shardlike skyscraper and Stefano Boeri's apartments with hanging gardens, the shiny new area between Porta Garibaldi and Porta Nuova is Milan's mini-Manhattan. Swanky Corso Como seamlessly links Corso Garibaldi with the emerging multicultural neighbourhood of Isola, making this a hot spot for bars, restaurants and cutting-edge shops.

The Sights in a Day

☀️ Start the day with a fascinating tour of Milan's **Cimitero Monumentale** (p73), final resting place of the great and the good. Begun in 1866 by Carlo Maciachini, the cemetery has evolved into a surreal open-air museum: home to more than 25 hectares of funerary monuments and fashionable mausoleums.

☀️ Pause for lunch at the rooftop bar of **Ceresio 7** (p74), where you could bed down for the day on a pool lounger, or opt instead for a food adventure at Viviana Varese's new Eataly restaurant, **Alice** (p73). Afterwards, if you haven't run mad amid the tempting food aisles, wander north enjoying the cruisey southern California vibe of Corso Como. Window-shop in fabulous **10 Corso Como** (p77) or hunt down modernist treasures in Isola at **Monica Castiglioni** (p77).

🌙 As evening falls, bar-hop around Isola to **Frida** (p75). **Les Pommes** (p74) and **Nordest Caffè** (p75). For dinner, fortify yourself with excellent Lombard fare at **Osteria del Treno** (p73), before embarking on a night of jazz at **Blue Note** (p76) or clubbing beneath the railway tracks at **Tunnel** (p76).

💜 **Best of Milan**

Architecture
Cimitero Monumentale (p73)

Stazione Centrale (p73)

Eating
Alice Ristorante (p73)

Osteria del Treno (p73)

Artico Gelateria (p74)

Drinking
Ceresio 7 (p74)

Cantine Isola (p75)

Frida (p75)

Nightlife
Tunnel (p76)

Blue Note (p76)

Getting There

Ⓜ **Metro** For the cemetery and the nightlife along Corso Como use Porta Garibaldi on the M2 (green line).

Ⓜ **Metro** For Isola use the new M5 (lilac line), which has convenient stops at Isola and Zara.

500 m
0.25 miles

ISOLA

Via Schiaparelli

13

Sondrio

Via Ponte Seveso

Via Sammartini

Stazione
Centrale

2

Centrale FS

Piazza di
Savoia

Piazza Duca
d'Aosta

Via Dom Vitruvio

Via Mauro
Macchi

Via Luigi Settembrini

V Napo Torriani

Via Vittor Pisani

Torre
Pirelli

Via Fabio Filzi

Via Giovanni Battista Pirelli

Via Generale
Gustavo Fara

Via Luigi Galvani

Via Melchiorre Gioia

Gioia

Via San Gregorio

Via Felice Casa

Viale Tur

3

Republica

Via G. Galilei

Viale della Liberazione

Via Giacomo Carissimi

Via Tonale

Via Luigi Galvani

Via Sebenico

Via Gaetano de Castillia

**UniCredit
Tower**

16

Piazza
Gae
Aulenti

Bastioni di Porta Nuova

Via Lario

Via F. Arese

Piazzale
Lagosta

11

15

Via
Garibaldi

Isola

Via F Confalonieri

12

**Stazione
Porta Garibaldi**

Garibaldi

17

19

Corso Como

Corso
Garibaldi

Via Thaön di Revel

Piazzale
Segrino

Via Borsieri

Via Pollaiuolo

Piazzale
Archinto

18

Via Jacopo
dal Verme

Via Pastrengo

6

Via Alessio di
Tocqueville

Via Bonnet

Piazzale XXV Aprile

Viale F Crispi

Via Cola
Montano

5

10

Piazza
Fidia

Via G. Pepe

Via Carmagnola

20

Via Tazzoli

Via Pasubio

Viale Pasubio

4

Via V
Civerchio

Via Alserio

Via A della Pergola

Via Carlo Farini

Bastioni di
Porta Volta

Viale Montello

Via Ceresio

7

CHINATOWN

Via Donato
Bramante

Via Paolo Sarpi

**Cimitero
Monumentale**

1

Piazzale
Cimitero
Monumentale

Via Giulio
Cesare
Procaccini

14

Via Messina

9

8

Via Valtellina

For reviews see	
◎ Sights	p73
⊗ Eating	p73
ⓓ Drinking	p74
⊕ Entertainment	p76
ⓖ Shopping	p76

Sights

Cimitero Monumentale CEMETERY

1 Map p72, A3

Behind striking Renaissance-revival black-and-white walls, Milan's wealthy have kept their dynastic ambitions alive long after death with grand sculptural gestures since 1866. Nineteenth-century death-and-the-maiden eroticism gives way to some fabulous abstract forms from midcentury masters. Studio BBPR's geometric steel-and-marble memorial to Milan's WWII concentration-camp dead sits in the centre, stark and moving. Grab a map inside the forecourt. (☏02 8846 5600; Piazzale Cimitero Monumentale; admission free; ⏱8am-6pm Tue-Sun; Ⓜ Monumentale)

Stazione Centrale ARCHITECTURE

2 Map p72, E3

Annually, nearly 100 million people pass through these hulking portals and onto train platforms beneath a cinematic cylindrical glass roof. Begun in 1912 but finally realised between 1925 and 1931, the station's extraordinary design is flush with the nationalist fervour that marked Mussolini's rule. Most of the overtly Fascist symbolism has been removed or obscured but the deco-tinged neo-Babylonian architecture can hardly hide its intent. (Piazza Duca d'Aosta; Ⓜ Centrale FS)

Eating

Alice Ristorante MODERN ITALIAN €€€

The restaurant of talented chef Viviana Varese and maître d', sommelier and fish expert Sandra Ciciriello, Alice is the pride of Eataly's new flagship foodstore (see 17 Map p72, C4). The top-floor views are a match for the superlative food on your plate and the menu is full of humour, with dishes such as Polp Fiction (octopus with zucchini trumpets) and That Ball! (truffle ice cream with chocolate, *zabaglione* – egg and marsala custard – and cocoa). (☏02 4949 7340; www.alice-ristorante.it; Eataly, Piazza XXV Aprile; meals €40-50; ⏱12.30-2.30pm & 7.30-10.30pm Mon-Sat; ✍; Ⓜ Moscova, Garibaldi)

Osteria del Treno ITALIAN €€

3 Map p72, E4

This Slow Food osteria with its Liberty-style ballroom is a piece of Milanese history, built originally as a club for railway workers at the nearby Stazione Centrale. Self-service lunches showcase a variety of Presidio-protected cheeses, cured meats and simple, authentic pasta dishes. Dinner is a more formal affair and on Sunday nights a *milonga* (tango dance) takes place in the ballroom. (☏02 670 04 79; www.osteriadeltreno.it; Via San Gregorio 46; meals €35; ⏱12.30-2.30pm & 8pm-midnight Mon-Fri, 8pm-midnight Sat & Sun; Ⓜ Centrale FS)

Antica Trattoria della Pesa

MILANESE €€€

4 ✗ Map p72, B4

Recipe for instant nostalgia: take the landmark building where Ho Chi Minh stayed in the '30s, add literary types from nearby publishing houses, mix with comfort food (osso buco on polenta topped with gremolata, *bollito misto* – boiled meat – and *cotoletta* – crumbed veal cutlets), spice it up with some red, and finish with a sigh over some smooth, boozy *zabaglione*. (📞02 655 57 41; www.anticatrattoriadellapesa.com; Viale Pasubio 10; meals €40-60; ⏱12.30-2.30pm & 7.30-11pm Mon-Sat; 🚊3, 4)

Artico Gelateria

GELATERIA €

5 ✗ Map p72, B2

All natural, hand-turned ice cream and sorbets in an interesting range of flavours such as chocolate with chilli, and DOP pistachio with salt and pepper. Watch them being made behind the counter while you wait your turn in the eager queue. (📞02 4549 4698; www.articogelateria.com; Via Porro Lambertenghi 15; 2 scoops €2.20; ⏱noon-11pm; 👶; Ⓜ Isola)

Les Pommes

INTERNATIONAL €€

6 ✗ Map p72, B3

Hankering after a hamburger and fries or a smoked-salmon bagel? Then the menu at Les Pommes is for you. Diners can choose from Scandinavian, American, Mediterranean or Italian menus, which include plenty of fresh fruit and salads alongside the bagels and burgers. Sunday brunch is packed out with a young, cool crowd. Come early. (📞02 8707 4765; www.lespommes.it; Via Pastrengo 7; meals €10-30; ⏱7.30am-10pm Mon-Sat, 9am-10pm Sun; Ⓜ Garibaldi)

Drinking

Ceresio 7

BAR

7 🍷 Map p72, A3

Heady views match the heady price of *aperitivo* at Milan's coolest rooftop bar, sitting atop the former 1930s Enel (electricity company) HQ. Two pools, two bars and a restaurant under the guidance of former Bulgari head chef Elio Sironi make this a hit with Milan's beautiful people. In the summer you can book a whole day by the pool from €110. (📞02 3103 9221; www.ceresio7.com; Via Ceresio 7; aperitivo €15, meals €60-80; ⏱12.30pm-1am; 🚊2, 4)

Alcatraz

CLUB

8 🍷 Map p72, B1

Founded by Italian rockstar Vasco Rossi, Alcatraz is now a multifunctional venue for live concerts, DJ sets, fashion shows and a weekly dance club. The 1800-sq-metre former garage space rocks to the sound of Latino, house and revival on Fridays and classic rock and roll on Saturdays. (📞02 6901 6352; www.alcatrazmilano.com; Via Valtellina 25; Ⓜ Isola, 🚊3, 4, 7, 11)

Cantine Isola

WINE BAR

9 Map p72, A4

Only octogenarians make use of the table at the back – everyone else hovers near the beautiful old bar, balancing plates of bruschetta and holding glasses at the ready to sample a selection of wines from 400 exceptional vintners. (☑ 02 331 52 49; Via Sarpi 30; ☷8.30am-9.30pm Tue-Sun; Ⓜ Garibaldi)

Frida

BAR

10 Map p72, B2

The jumble of tables in the heated courtyard and the comfy couches inside make it easy to bond over beer or regional wine with an arty crowd. The *aperitivo* spread is continuously replenished and sports plenty of veg dishes. No pretensions, no entourages, just good music, good value and good times. (☑ 02 68 02 60; www.fridaisola.it; Via Pollaiuolo 3; ☷12.30-3pm & 6pm-2am; Ⓜ Zara, Garibaldi)

Nordest Caffè

BAR

11 Map p72, C2

So laid-back you might have trouble getting served, this sunny cafe-bar invites long, lazy afternoons. The young, local crowd have such a thing down to an art, especially on Sundays for live jazz and brunch from midday. (☑ 02 6900 1910; Via Borsieri 35; ☷8am-9pm Mon, to 11.30pm Tue-Sat, 8.30am-9pm Sun; ☐; Ⓜ Garibaldi, Zara)

JACOPO RAULE / GETTY IMAGES ©

Alcatraz

RED

CAFE

12 Map p72, C3

RED stands for Read, Eat, Dream and is the latest initiative from savvy Italian publisher and bookseller Feltrinelli. Aimed at attracting younger, iPad-touting customers, RED is a concept-cafe-cum-restaurant housed in the newest Feltrinelli bookshop situated amid the skyscrapers on Piazza Gae Aulenti. At night, book browsers can enjoy the spectacularly lit landscape or challenge each other to games of table football. (☑ 02 6558 0153; Piazza Gae Aulenti 1; ☷7.30am-11pm Mon-Fri, 10am-midnight Sat, to 11pm Sun; ☐; Ⓜ Garibaldi)

Tunnel
CLUB

13 🚇 Map p72, E2

A landmark of Milan's alternative scene, Tunnel takes its moniker as top underground club seriously and is literally housed in a tunnel beneath the rail tracks of the Stazione Centrale. Friday night's Le Cannibale features indie acts and electronic, while Saturday evenings attract top DJs from the techno scene, such as Ellen Alien, Nina Kraviz, Nicolaar Jaar and Ame & Dixon. (www.tunnel-milano.it; Via Sammartini 30; admission €15-25; ⏰11pm-5am Wed-Sat; Ⓜ Centrale)

Local Life
Chinatown

Milan's Chinatown is centred on Via Paolo Sarpi and Via Donato Bramante. The Chinese community has deep roots in the city and is the oldest in Italy. More-recent arrivals mix with families that settled here in the 1920s and '30s. While Milan likes to think of itself as Italy's most multicultural city, casual racism or the flippant fetishism of fashion-land can be the most common response to questions of ethnic identity. But hard work and harmony is the usual order of the day. Chinatown is a good shopping alternative: pick up bargain clothing, leatherwear and electrical goods, as well as Asian produce. Most restaurants here specialise in Zhejiang cuisine.

Entertainment

La Fabbrica del Vapore
PERFORMING ARTS

14 ⭐ Map p72, A3

This industrial site once housed a factory for electric trams; now it lends its vast warehouses to a centre of the arts particularly aimed at developing the creative skills of young people. Dance, photography, theatre, cinema and concerts fill the factory's program year-round. (www.fabbricadelvapore.org; Via Procaccini 4; 👥; 🚋7, 12, 14)

Blue Note
JAZZ

15 ⭐ Map p72, C2

Top-class jazz acts from around the world perform here at the only European outpost for New York's Blue Note jazz club. If you haven't prebooked you can buy tickets at the door from 7.30pm. It also does a popular easy-listening Sunday brunch (€35 per adult, or €70 for two adults and two children under 12). (📞02 6901 6888; www.bluenotemilano.com; Via Borsieri 37; tickets €22-40; ⏰7.30pm-midnight Tue-Sun Sep-Jun, brunch noon Sun Oct-Mar; Ⓜ Isola, Zara)

Shopping

Ziio
JEWELLERY

16 🔒 Map p72, C3

Elizabeth Paradon's unique handworked jewellery is coveted the world over by celebrities and fashionistas. Combining micro Murano glass beads, gold, silver and semiprecious stones, lapis, pearls, jade and coral, the bold and colourful creations are influenced by decorative motifs from Venice, Greece, Egypt and the Far East. (☑02 3670 6771; www.ziio. eu; Via Gaetano di Castillia 20; ☻10.30am-2.15pm & 3-7.30pm Tue-Fri, 11am-2.30pm & 3-7.30pm Sat, 2-6pm Sun & Mon; Ⓜ Garibaldi)

Eataly
FOOD

17 🔒 Map p72, C4

Alongside New York and Tokyo, Milan now has a flagship branch of artisan food purveyor Eataly. The revamped Teatro Smeraldo seems a fitting venue to showcase dazzling wares, from Italian craft beers to specialist gelato from Làit. Live music tinkles as you attend cookery courses. If you don't overdo the tastings, head upstairs to gourmet restaurant Alice (p73). (☑02 4949 7301; www.eataly.it; Piazza XXV Aprile 10; ☻10am-midnight; Ⓜ Moscova, Garbaldi)

Monica Castiglioni
JEWELLERY

18 🔒 Map p72, C3

Daughter of famous industrial designer Achille Castiglioni, Monica Castiglioni has a deep understanding of materials and proportions. To this she adds her own unique vision, turning out organic, industrial-style jewellery in bronze, silver and gold using an ancient lost-wax casting technique. (☑02 8723 7979; www.monicacastiglioni.com; Via Pastrengo 4; ☻11am-8pm Thu-Sat; Ⓜ Garibaldi)

10 Corso Como
FASHION

19 🔒 Map p72, C4

This might be the world's most hyped 'concept shop', but Carla Sozzani's selection of desirable things (Lanvin ballet flats, Alexander Girard wooden dolls, a demicouture frock by a designer you've not read about *yet*) makes 10 Corso Como a fun window-shopping experience. There's a bookshop upstairs with art and design titles, and a hyperstylish bar and restaurant in the main atrium and picture-perfect courtyard. (☑02 2900 2674; www.10corsocomo.com; Corso Como 10; ☻10.30am-7.30pm Tue & Fri-Sun, to 9pm Wed & Thu, 3.30-7.30pm Mon; Ⓜ Garibaldi)

10 Corso Como Outlet
FASHION

20 🔒 Map p72, B3

At the back of a sunny courtyard, you'll find a surprisingly serene outlet store. There are genuine bargains on big names such as Marni, Prada and Comme, and even better discounts on quirkier pieces such as Stephen Jones hats. Menswear is particularly strong. (☑02 2900 2674; www.10corsocomo.com; Via Tazzoli 3; ☻1-7pm Fri, 11am-7pm Sat & Sun; Ⓜ Garibaldi, 🚊3, 4)

Explore

Corso Magenta & Sant'Ambrogio

Leonardo da Vinci's *The Last Supper* and the Basilica di Sant'Ambrogio draw visitors to these leafy streets, but there's an equal mix of sacred and secular here. Bourgeois bolthole Via Vincenzo Monti is lined with restaurants and shops; to the south the Museo Nazionale della Scienza e della Tecnologia rings with the chatter of young explorers; and Bramante's cloisters fill with students at the sprawling Università Cattolica.

The Sights in a Day

A coffee and *cornetto* (croissant) at **Biffi** (p85) marks the start of the day. Then, fully fortified, head to the **Museo Nazionale della Scienza e della Tecnologia** (p83) for a morning marvelling at models of Leonardo's machines alongside fascinating exhibits on music, astrology, horology, metallurgy, ballistics, aeronautics and transport.

Grab a gourmet *panino* and beer with locals at **De Santis** (p84) and toss a coin for your next stop: the golden sky and St Ambrogio's tomb at Milan's most important **basilica** (p83), or Bernardino Luini's heavenly frescoes at the **Chiesa di San Maurizio** (p83), including a quick lesson in the city's history at the adjoining **Civico Museo Archeologico** (p83).

With your prebooked evening ticket for **The Last Supper** (p80) tucked safely in your pocket, stop for a leisurely glass of wine and platter of *aperitivo* (see p97) goodies at **Boccascena Café** (p85) before hotfooting it to gaze on Leonardo da Vinci's masterful mural in the refectory of Santa Maria delle Grazie. A guided tour or audio guide is well worth the investment. Finish the day with a romantic dinner at **La Brisa** (p84).

◉ Top Sights

The Last Supper (p80)

♥ Best of Milan

History

Basilica di Sant'Ambrogio (p83)

Civico Museo Archeologico (p83)

Leonardo da Vinci

The Last Supper (p80)

Museo Nazionale della Scienza e della Tecnologia (p83)

Eating

La Brisa (p84)

Buongusto (p84)

De Santis (p84)

Shopping

Galleria L'Affiche (p86)

Risi (p86)

MUST Shop (p87)

Getting There

Ⓜ **Metro** For Museo Nazionale della Scienza e della Tecnologia and Basilica di Sant'Ambrogio use Sant'Ambrogio on M2 (green line).

Ⓜ **Metro** M1 stop Cadorna is best for *The Last Supper,* Civico Museo Archeologico and San Maurizio.

Top Sights
The Last Supper

Milan's most famous painting, Leonardo da Vinci's *The Last Supper*, is hidden away on a wall of the refectory adjoining the Basilica di Santa Maria delle Grazie. Depicting Christ and his disciples at the dramatic moment when Christ reveals he is aware of the betrayal afoot, it is a masterful psychological study and one of the world's most iconic images.

👁 Map p82, C2

Piazza Santa Maria delle Grazie 2

adult/reduced €8/4.75

🕐 8.15am-7pm Tue-Sun

Ⓜ Cadorna

The Last Supper by Leonardo da Vinci

Don't Miss

The Last Supper

When Leonardo was at work on *The Last Supper,* a star-struck monk noted that he would sometimes arrive in the morning, stare at yesterday's effort, then promptly call it quits for the day. Your visit too will be similarly brief (15 minutes to be exact), but the baggage of a thousand dodgy reproductions are quickly shed once face to face with the luminous work itself. The experimental techniques used by da Vinci and years of abuse have left the mural fragile, but its condition does nothing to lessen its astonishing beauty and enthralling psychological drama.

Basilica di Santa Maria delle Grazie

Any visit to *The Last Supper* should be accompanied by a tour of the **Basilica di Santa Maria delle Grazie** (www.grazieop.it; Piazza Santa Maria delle Grazie; ⊙7am-noon & 3-7.30pm Mon-Sat, 7.30am-12.30pm & 3.30-9pm Sun; Ⓜ Cadorna, 🚊16), a Unesco World Heritage Site. Designed by Guiniforte Solari, with later additions by Bramante, the basilica encapsulates the magnificence of the Milanese court of Ludovico 'il Moro' Sforza and Beatrice d'Este. Articulated in fine brickwork and terracotta, the building is robust but fanciful, its apse topped by Bramante's cupola and its interior lined with frescoes.

Codex Atlanticus

The *Codex Atlanticus* is the largest collection of da Vinci's drawings in the world. More than 1700 of them were gathered by sculptor Pompeo Leoni in 12 volumes, so heavy they threatened the preservation of the drawings themselves. The sheets have now been unbound and are displayed in softly lit glass cases in Bramante's frescoed **Sagrestia Monumentale** (www.leonardo-ambrosiana.it; Via Caradosso 1; adult/reduced €10/8; ⊙8.30am-7pm Tue-Sun, 9am-1pm & 2-6pm Mon; Ⓜ Cadorna, 🚊16).

☑ Top Tips

▶ Reservations for *The Last Supper* must be made weeks, if not months, in advance. Or you can take a city tour with **Autostradale** (www.autostradale.it; Piazza Castello 1; tickets €65; ⊙Tue-Sun), which includes a visit.

▶ Once booked, you'll be allotted a strict visiting time. If you're late, your ticket will be resold.

▶ Multilingual guided tours (€3.50) are offered and need to be reserved in advance.

✖ Take a Break

Grab a quick coffee or beer with locals at Bar Magenta (p86).

Follow Leonardo's divine dining experience with an atmospheric dinner in 17th-century Taverna Moriggi (p84).

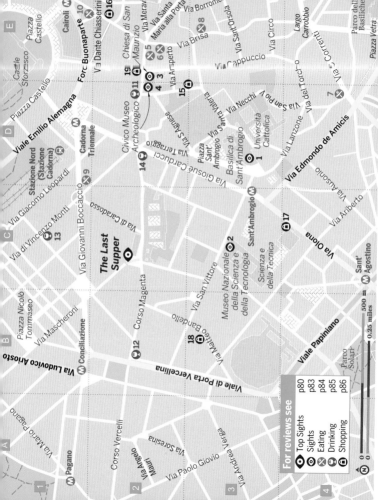

For reviews see
Top Sights   p80
Sights   p83
Eating   p84
Drinking   p85
Shopping   p86

500 m
0.25 miles

Sights

Basilica di Sant'Ambrogio
BASILICA

1 ◎ Map p82, D3

St Ambrose, Milan's patron saint and one-time superstar bishop, is buried in the crypt of this red-brick cathedral, which he founded in AD 379. It's a fitting legacy, built and rebuilt with a purposeful simplicity that is truly uplifting: the seminal Lombard Romanesque basilica. Shimmering altar mosaics and a biographical 835 AD golden altarpiece, which once served as the cladding for the saint's sarcophagus, light up the shadowy vaulted interior. (☑02 8645 0895; www.basilicasantambrogio.it; Piazza Sant'Ambrogio 15; ⊙10am-noon & 2.30-6pm Mon-Sat, 3-5pm Sun; Ⓜ Sant'Ambrogio)

Museo Nazionale della Scienza e della Tecnologia
MUSEUM

2 ◎ Map p82, C3

Kids, would-be inventors and geeks will go goggle-eyed at Milan's impressive museum of science and technology, the largest of its kind in Italy. It is a fitting tribute in a city where arch-inventor Leonardo da Vinci did much of his finest work. The 16th-century monastery where it is housed features a collection of more than 10,000 items, including models based on da Vinci's engineering sketches, and outdoor hangars housing steam trains, planes, full-sized galleons and Italy's first submarine, *Enrico Toti*. (☑02 48 55 51; www.museoscienza.org; Via San Vittore 21; adult/child €10/7, submarine tours €8; ⊙9.30am-5pm Tue-Fri, to 6.30pm Sat & Sun; ♿; Ⓜ Sant'Ambrogio)

Chiesa di San Maurizio
CHURCH

3 ◎ Map p82, E2

The 16th-century royal chapel and convent of San Maurizio is Milan's hidden crown jewel, every inch of it covered in breathtaking frescoes, several of them executed by Bernardino Luini, who worked with Leonardo. Many of the frescoes immortalise Ippolita Sforza, Milanese literary maven, and other members of the powerful Sforza clan. (Corso Magenta 15; ⊙9.30am-5.30pm Tue-Sat, 1.30-5.30pm Sun; Ⓜ Cadorna)

Civico Museo Archeologico
MUSEUM

4 ◎ Map p82, D2

The 8th-century Monastero Maggiore, once the most important Benedictine convent in the city, is now home to Milan's archaeological museum. Access is via a cloister, where fragments of the city's Roman walls can be seen. Ground-floor rooms display important artefacts from Roman Mediolanum (which later became Milan), while on upper floors the city's history unfolds in well-curated collections of Etruscan, Greek, Gothic and Lombard artefacts. In the garden the 3rd-century frescoed **Ansperto Tower** marks the limits of Mediolanum's city walls. (☑02 8844 5208; www.comune.milano.it/museoarcheologico; Corso Magenta 15; adult/child €5/3; ⊙9am-5.30pm Tue-Sun; Ⓜ Cadorna)

Local Life
San Siro Stadium

The city's two football clubs, AC Milan and FC Internazionale Milano (aka Inter), play on alternate weeks between October and May at the iconic **San Siro Stadium** (www.sansiro.net; Piazzale Angelo Moratti; M San Siro). The cross-town derby between the two – which takes place twice a year (in spring and autumn) – known as the Milan Derby or the Derby della Madonnina, is one of the greatest rivalries in the Italian League. Serie A fans can visit the **Museo Inter e Milan** (02 404 24 32; www.sansiro.net; Via Piccolomini 5, Gate 21; museum & tour adult/reduced €17/12; 9.30am-6pm; M Lotto, 16, shuttle from Piazzale Lotto to stadium) for nonstop screenings of matches, memorabilia and trophies galore.

Eating

De Santis

SANDWICHES €

5 Map p82, E2

Sandwiches here are so damn good you may eschew restaurant dining just to sample that *panini* with prosciutto, spicy goat cheese, pepperoni, aubergine and artichokes. The more than 200 variations on the menu and De Santis' decades of experience are good reasons why punters are prepared to queue at this tiny venue. Beer is served on tap to the lucky few who find seating. (www.paninidesantis.it; Corso Magenta 9; sandwiches €6-8; noon-11.30pm; M Cadorna)

La Brisa

MODERN ITALIAN €€€

6 Map p82, E2

Discreet, elegant and exquisitely romantic. Push open the screened door and the maître d' will guide you to a table beneath centuries-old linden trees in a secluded courtyard, where ivy climbs the walls and pink hydrangeas bob in the breeze. Chef Antonio Facciolo's seasonal menus are similarly elegant, his signature dish a mouthwatering roast pork in a myrtle-berry drizzle. (02 8645 0521; www.ristorantelabrisa.it; Via Brisa 15; meals €50-70; 12.45-2.30pm & 7.45-10.30pm Mon-Fri, 7.45-10.30pm Sun; M Cairoli, Cordusio)

Buongusto

MODERN ITALIAN €€

7 Map p82, D4

Come for daringly original dishes such as pumpkin ravioli on 'iced' parsley that melts in your mouth; or steak tartare with anchovies, capers and 'snow butter'. Knowledgable, multilingual staff will guide you through the menu, or opt for the Surprise Menu (€70). Don't leave without trying the olive pound cake, a chocolate cake made with black olives and *fleur de sel*. (02 8645 2479; www.buongusto.eu; Via Caminadella 2; meals €35-40; noon-3pm & 6.30pm-midnight Tue-Sat; 2, 14)

Taverna Moriggi

MILANESE €€

8 Map p82, E3

In a city devoted to the now and the next, this taverna stands stoically apart in a 17th-century structure. Wrought-iron candelabras cast a gentle light over checked tablecloths and walls left to distress characterfully over the decades. The menu is short and traditional: saffron risotto, hearty osso buco and veal with polenta. In autumn you can catch live jazz on Tuesday nights. (📞02 8058 2007; www.tavernamoriggi.com; Via Morigi 8; meals €25-35; 🕙noon-2.30pm & 7.45-10.30pm Mon-Sat; 🚇16, 27)

Shockolat
GELATERIA €

9 🍴 Map p82, D1

As its name suggests, this gelateria plays flavour favourites. Variations on the chocolate theme include milk, dark, white, chilli, *gianduja* (chocolate-hazelnut) and cinnamon. People have been known to eat a *panini* or a slice of homemade cake here, but the crowds that queue out the door come for the cups and cones. (📞02 4810 0597; www.shockolat. it; Via Boccaccio 9; small/medium/large cup €2.50/3/3.50; 🕙7.30-1am; ❄️♿; 🇲Cadorna)

Da Rita e Antonio
PIZZA €

10 🍴 Map p82, E1

Serving the neighbourhood since 1972, this restaurant continues to do exactly what it's always done: soft, fluffy Neapolitan pizza with a raised rim that tenderly cradles toppings of gooey mozzarella from Prati del Volturno dairy, spicy salami and anchovies with Sicilian capers. Other dishes such as homemade gnocchi feature on the menu, but why mess with a perfect recipe? (📞02 87 55 79; http://daritaeantonio.it; Via Giacomo Puccini 2; pizzas €6.50-9; 🕙noon-3pm & 7pm-midnight Tue Fri & Sun, 6pm midnight Sat; ♿; 🇲Cairoli)

Drinking

Boccascena Café
BAR

11 🍷 Map p82, D2

Actors and artists mill around tables, anticipating or reviewing the evening's entertainment at Teatro Litta, an 18th-century *palazzo* (mansion) with a charming courtyard and clock tower. In the Teatro's grand foyer, Boccascena presents drinks with a flourish, dramatically lit by mod chrome chandeliers. Unscripted dialogue and much levity ensues; the end is up to you. (Corso Magenta 24; 🕙10am-4pm Mon, 10am-4pm & 6-9pm Tue-Fri, 6-9pm Sat & Sun; 🇲Cadorna)

Biffi Pasticceria
CAFE

12 🍷 Map p82, B2

Proud keepers of a traditional *panetùn* (panettone) recipe that once pleased Pope Pius X, Biffi has changed little since its 1847 opening. With its polished walnut bar and Murano chandeliers, its air of old-world elegance continues to attract the good people of Milan, who come to meet over dainty cream cakes, coffee and cocktails. (📞02 4800 6702; www.biffipasticceria.it; Corso Magenta 87; 🕙7am-8.30pm; ♿; 🇲Conciliazione)

Pasticceria Leonardo
CAFE, BAR

13   Map p82, C1

Perfect, silky cappuccinos and light breakfast brioche kick off the day at this popular cafe just off fancy Via Vincenzo Monti. Midmorning, the crowd moves on to *spritz* (prosecco cocktail) with *tramezzini* (sandwiches); for lunch, focaccia Genovese and a glass of wine, then tea with berry tarts. Finally, come 6pm, the crowd swells for cocktails at outdoor seating that perfectly catches the sinking sun. (02 439 03 02; Via Aurelio Saffi 7; 7am-11pm; Cadorna)

Bar Magenta
BAR

14   Map p82, D2

Grab a seat in this historic bar and let Milan come to you. Drift in during the day for espresso, sandwiches and beer, or join the students during early evening for wine from a tap. (02 805 38 08; http://barmagenta.jimdo.com; Via Giosué Carducci 13; 8am-7.30pm Mon-Wed & Sun, to 10.30pm Thu, to 2am Fri & Sat; Cadorna)

Shopping

Galleria L'Affiche
ARTS

15   Map p82, D2

A treasure trove of vintage posters, fine-art prints, playbills and photographs, Galleria L'Affiche has a cult following and loyal stable of artists who entrust it with some of their finest work. Invest a few euros in some kitsch vintage postcards or spend several hundreds on a collectible; either way, you'll have hours of fun here. (02 8645 0124; www.affiche.it; Via Nirone 11; 2.30-8pm Mon, 10am-8pm Tue-Sat; 16)

Risi
FASHION

16   Map p82, E2

Head to Risi for a dose of effortless Milanese chic. Here you can stock up on soft grey and white linen shirts and trousers; honeycomb polo shirts in sober colours; and comfortable beachwear in classic pinstripes. Season-appropriate weights and wefts and an absence of logos mean you'll blend in with the natives. (02 8909 2185; www.risimilano.com; Via San Giovanni sul Muro 21; 3-7.30pm Mon, 10am-2.30pm & 3-7.30pm Tue-Sat; Cairoli)

Understand
Painter at Court

With his *Portrait of a Young Man* (c 1486) and portraits of Ludovico's mistresses, *Lady with the Ermine* (c 1489) and *La Belle Ferronière* (c 1490), Leonardo da Vinci transformed the rigid conventions of portraiture to depict highly individual images imbued with effortless naturalism. Then he evolved concepts of idealised proportions and the depiction of internal emotional states (*St Jerome*; c 1488), which all cohered in his masterpiece, *The Last Supper*.

PAOLO CORDELLI / GETTY IMAGES ©

Spazio Rossana Orlandi

MUST Shop

MUSEUM SHOP

17 Map p82, C4

The science museum's fabulous concept shop is *the* place to go for science-inspired books, design items, gadgets and games. Personal favourites include submarine bath lights, Corker robots made out of wine corks, and the star theatre planetarium that allows you to beam the heavens onto a ceiling near you. Access to the shop is through the museum or via Via Olona. (02 4855 5340; www.mustshop.it; Via Olona 6; 10am-7pm Tue-Sun; Sant'Ambrogio)

Spazio Rossana Orlandi

HOMEWARES

18 Map p82, B3

Installed in a former tie factory in the Magenta district, this iconic interior-design studio is a challenge to find. Once inside, though, it's hard to leave the dreamlike treasure trove stacked with vintage and contemporary limited-edition pieces from young and upcoming artists. (02 46 74 47; www.rossanaorlandi.com; Via Matteo Bandello 14; 3-7pm Mon, 10am-7pm Tue-Sat; Sant'Ambrogio)

Local Life
Zona Tortona

Getting There

M **Metro** Take the M2 (green line) to Porta Genova. Then cross the Graffiti Bridge to the left of the station as you exit.

Once a tangle of working-class tenements and factories, Zona Tortona is now flush with design companies, studios and neighbourhood eateries. This is home to the head offices of Diesel and Armani (look for the Tadao Ando–designed Armani Teatro on Via Bergognone). During April's Salone del Mobile (Furniture Fair), the area hosts satellite shows, launches and parties, transforming into a destination in itself.

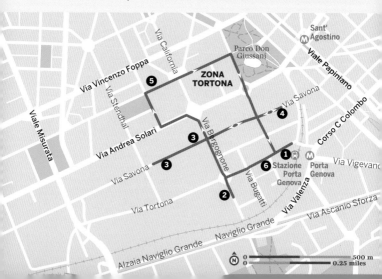

1 Coffee at Cafè del Binari

Named after the railway tracks that drove modernity through the heart of Milan, Liberty-style **Cafè del Binari** (Via Tortona 3; ⏱8am-5.15pm; Ⓜ Porta Genova) reflects all the glitz and the glamour that the railway age promised. Plump red tub chairs, a carved mahogany bar and elaborate tiled and stencilled walls immediately transport you to a more gracious age.

2 Armani Silos

When Italian *Vogue* art director Flavio Lucchini opened a photographic studio on scruffy Via Tortona in 1983, everyone thought he was mad. But now 'the zone' is a magnet for designers, artists and photographers. No wonder Giorgio Armani decided to locate his new legacy museum, **Armani Silos** (☎02 9163 0010; www.armanisilos. com; Via Bergognone 40; adult/reduced €12/8.40; ⏱11am-8pm Tue, Wed, Fri & Sun, to 10pm Thu & Sat; Ⓜ Porta Genova), here.

3 Fashionable Lunches

Lunching in the neighbourhood of a picky design crowd has its benefits; Zona Tortona is full of highly imaginative, quality restaurants. Notable among them are vegetarian-friendly **Al Fresco** (☎02 4953 3630; www.lafres-comilano.it; Via Savona 50; meals €30-40; ⏱12.30-3.30pm & 7.30pm-1am; 🍴; Ⓜ Porta Genova, 🚋14) and funky '50s bistro **Angelo's** (☎02 455 48 64; www.angelos.it; Via Savona 55; meals €15-25; ⏱12.30-2.45pm & 7.30-10.30pm Mon-Sat; 🚋14), best for brunch and light fusion lunches.

4 Design Library

There's no better place to soak up the arty vibe of Tortona than the **Design Library Café** (☎02 8942 3329; www. designlibrary.it; Via Savona 11; meals €15-20; ⏱7.30am-10.30pm Mon, to 11.30pm Tue-Thu, to 2am Fri, 5pm-2am Sat; 🌸; Ⓜ Porta Genova). Home to a cool crowd of designers, architects and fashion students tapping away on their MacBook Airs, the library (yearly membership €25) is a design-buff's dream.

5 Concept Shopping

Brainchild of Sardinian fashion designer Antonio Marras, **Nonostantemarras** (☎02 7628 0991; www. nonostantemarras.it; Via Cola di Rienzo 8; ⏱10am-7pm Tue-Sat; 🚋14) is an eccentric concept store hidden in an ivy-draped courtyard. It's full of magpie artefacts and books that sit alongside Marras' creative, colourful high-fashion clothing. Come here to find something unique, have a cup of tea or simply enjoy the magical space.

6 Designer Drinks

During Salone del Mobile, the whole of Zona Tortona turns into an outdoor bar and party venue thanks to the fringe fair, **Fuorisalone** (http://fuorisalone.it; ⏱Apr). During the fair, daily exhibits, events and parties are staged at Superstudio Più on Via Tortona 27, while the international design set piles into hyper-styled bars such as **Les Gitanes** (www. lesgitanesbistrot.it; Via Forcella 2a; cocktails €8-10; ⏱8am-midnight Mon-Thu, to 2am Fri, 6.30pm-2am Sat; Ⓜ Porta Genova).

Explore

Navigli

The Navigli neighbourhood is named after its most identifiable feature – the canals. Designed as the motorways of medieval Milan, they powered the city's fortunes until the railroads, WWII bombs and neglect brought about their closure in the 1970s. These days they provide a scenic backdrop to the bookshops, boutiques and bars that make this Milan's most kicking bohemian 'burb.

The Sights in a Day

 Breakfast on superior pastries at **Gattullo** (p92) then wander west to gaze on the treasures of the **Portinari chapel** (p95), and over the revamped dock and market beside Piazza XXIV Maggio. From here the Naviglio Grande and Pavese canals stretch southwards; grab a cycle-share bike and explore or hop aboard one of the **Navigli Lombardi** (p93) barges for a one-hour tour.

If you return early enough, lunch at Slow Food–recommended **Le Vigne** (p96) or the **Mercato Metropolitano** (p96). Then browse the funky shops along Ripa di Porta Ticinese. As the afternoon wanes, window-shop your way up to the **San Lorenzo Columns** (p95) for an ice cream from **Gelateria le Colonne** (p97). There might be a busker in the piazza to serenade you.

The evening is just getting going about now, so after a quick drink at retro **Cuore** (p98) head back down to the Naviglio Grande and bar-hop from **Mag Café** (p97) to **Ugo** (p97), ending up at **Fonderie Milanesi** (p93) or alternative club **Cox 18** (p93).

For a local's day on the canals in Navigli, see p92.

Local Life
Life on the Canals (p92)

Best of Milan

Eating
Gattullo (p92)

Langosteria 10 (p95)

Le Vigne (p96)

Basara (p95)

Drinking
Mag Café (p97)

Fonderie Milanesi (p93)

Bar Rita (p93)

Entertainment
Cox 18 (p93)

Auditorium di Milano (p98)

Nibada Theatre (p99)

Getting There

M Metro Porta Genova on M2 (green line) is the closest stop for Via Vigevano and the Naviglio Grande.

Tram Use tram 3 for the shops along Corso di Porta Ticinese, Piaza XXIV Maggio and the Alzaia Naviglio Pavese canal.

Tram 9 from Porta Genova travels east down Via Vigevano and Viale Col di Lana.

Local Life
Life on the Canals

Ever since the Renaissance the warehouses and factories lining Milan's canals have been a hive of creative and commercial endeavour. Locals love the area for weekend shopping and canalside drinking and dining. Post Expo, the area looks better than ever with revamped pedestrian walkways, new cycle paths and the restored centerpiece, the historic dock.

1 Breakfast at Gattullo

Rise early to get the best of the bountiful pastry bar at **Gattullo** (⌚02 5831 0497; www.gattullo.it; Piazzale di Porta Lodovico 2; pastries from €1.50; ⏰7am-9pm Sep-Jul; ✳✦; ⬛3, 9) before locals devour all the myrtle-berry croissants and delicate *sfogliatelle* (layered flaky pastries) stuffed with divine chantilly cream. At weekends locals stand five deep at the bar, so take a seat in the salon and gaze at the counter of

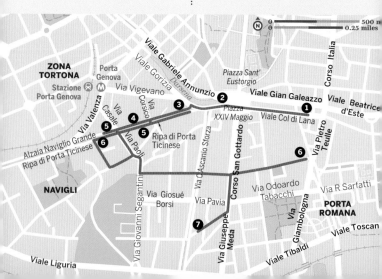

cakes and the surreal 1970s Murano chandeliers.

2 Hanging Out at the Darsena

One of the best legacies of Expo 2015 is Milan's revamped *darsena* (dock). Once the city's main port, located at the confluence of Naviglio Grande and Pavese, it has now been transformed into a tree-lined pedestrian piazza, with dockside **Nuovo Mercato Ticinese** (Piazza XXIV Maggio; ⊘8.30am-1pm & 4-8pm Tue-Sat; Ⓜ Porta Genova, ⊟3) food market and a grassy park with a kids play area.

3 Boat Tours

Canals were the autostradas of medieval Milan, transporting lumber, marble, salt, oil and wine into town. The largest of them, the Naviglio Grande, grew from an irrigation ditch to become one of the city's busiest thoroughfares in the late 13th century. From April to September you can take a boat tour along it with **Navigli Lombardi** (⊘02 667 91 31; www.naviglilombardi.it; Alzaia Naviglio Grande 4; adult €8-12; ⊘Apr-Sep; Ⓜ Porta Genova, ⊟3).

4 Neighbourhood Market

Come the last Sunday of the month you'll find the **Mercatone dell'Antiquariato** (www.navigliogrande.mi.it; Alzaia Naviglio Grande; ⊘9am-6pm last Sun of month; Ⓜ Porta Genova) set up along a 2km stretch of the Naviglio Grande. With more than 400 well-vetted antique and secondhand traders, it provides hours of treasure-hunting pleasure.

5 Browsing

With its old warehouses and low rents, Navigli is home to a thriving community of artists and musicians. Their eclectic studios line the canals. Join locals browsing for classic vinyl at **Dischivolanti** (⊘02 8940 1623; Ripa di Porta Ticinese 47; ⊘10am-1pm & 3-7.45pm Mon-Thu, to midnight Fri & Sat, 2-8pm Sun; Ⓜ Porta Genova) or artful comics and posters at **SuperGulp** (⊘02 837 22 16; www.supergulp.net; Alzaia Naviglio Grande 54; ⊘10am-1pm & 3pm-midnight; Ⓜ Porta Genova).

6 Aperitivo

On weekend and summer evenings, Milanese from all over the city come for Navigli's *aperitivo* (see p97) scene. Almost every bar along the Naviglio Grande offers an *aperitivo* buffet, but locals swear by **Bar Rita** (⊘02 83 28 65; Via Fumagalli 1; cocktails €5-9; ⊘6.30pm-2am Mon-Sat; Ⓜ Porta Genova) and cool, converted metal foundry **Fonderie Milanesi** (www.fonderiemilanesi.it; Via Giovenale 7; aperitivo €8; ⊘7pm-2am; ⊟15).

7 Clubbing

Much like Paris' Left Bank or London's Soho, Navigli is the indisputable hub of Milan's *movida* (nightlife) scene. A long-time favourite of the Milanese *movida*, **Cox 18** (www.cox18.noblogs.org; Via Conchetta 18; Ⓜ Romolo) is a self-managed community space tucked behind an awesome piece of graffiti by street artist Blu. Evening offerings include concerts, alternative bands, debates and exhibitions.

Sights

Basilica di San Lorenzo BASILICA

1 Map p94, C1

It's difficult not to be bowled over by this oft-ignored hotchpotch jumble of towers, lodges, apses and domes. In spite of appearances, it really is the one basilica. At its heart is an early-Christian circular structure with three adjoining octagonal chapels, dating to the 4th century. What's left of a Romanesque atrium leads to the heart of the church and before it stand 16 Roman columns, now a primary hang-out for kissing teens. (www.sanlorenzomaggiore.com; Corso di Porta Ticinese 39; ⏰8am-6.30pm Mon-Sat, 9am-7pm Sun; 🚋2, 14)

San Lorenzo Columns ARCHAEOLOGICAL SITE

2 Map p94, C1

The free-standing row of 16 Corinthian columns from Milan's Mediolanum heyday were salvaged from a crumbling Roman residence and lined up here to form the portico of the new church. Their pagan spirit lingers; welcome to what is the site of many an evening's beery indulgence. (Corso di Porta Ticinese; 🚋2, 14)

Basilica di Sant'Eustorgio BASILICA

3 Map p94, C2

Built in the 4th century to house the bones of the Three Kings, Sant'Eustorgio is one of Milan's oldest churches. Its harmonious exterior belies its rabble-rousing past as Milan's Inquisition HQ, but the real draw is Pigello Portinari's private **chapel** (adult/reduced €6/3; ⏰10am-6pm; 🚋2, 3, 9). Representative of the Medici bank in Milan, Portinari had the cash to splash on Milan's finest Renaissance chapel, built in Gothic style and frescoed with masterpieces by Vincenzo Foppa. (Piazza Sant'Eustorgio; ⏰7.45am-6.30pm; 🚋2, 3, 9)

Eating

Basara SUSHI €€€

4 Map p94, A2

Making a name for yourself in Milan's sophisticated sushi scene isn't easy, but chef Hiro's lobster maki roll sings a siren song that packs this place out for two sittings every evening. The raw-fish plates are superb, particularly the pretty block of red Sicilian shrimps served on a black slate slab with a sprinkle of sea salt. (📞02 5811 1649; www.basaramilano.it; Via Tortona 12; meals €50-70; ⏰8.30am-3.30pm & 7pm-12.30am Mon-Sat, Ⓜ Porta Genova)

Langosteria 10 Bistrot & Bottega SEAFOOD €€

5 Map p94, A2

Take a pew at the marble-topped bar of this Parisian-style bistro and order a glass of champagne to accompany your oysters or Alaskan king-crab

cocktails €8; ⏰8.30-3am Mon-Fri, 5pm-3am Sat, 8.30am-3pm Sun; Porta Genova)

Cuore

BAR

15 Map p94, C1

Retro Cuore has heart and soul by the bucketload with its vintage '50s furniture, TVs screening cult films, and *Hawaii Five-O* cocktails including piña coladas and mai tais garnished with floral bouquets. It's popular with students from the Sacro Cuore university and the laid-back *aperitivo* includes a vegan option on request. (📞02 5811 8311; www.cuoremilano.it; Via Mora 3; cocktails €5-8; ⏰6pm-2am; 🚊2, 14)

Sacrestia Famacia Alcolica

BAR

16 Map p94, B4

Retaining its theatrical character, this one-time bordello, converted by the Curia into a pharmacy, now serves 'alchemical' cocktails for the pleasure of its punters. Sip fortifying mojitos amid the surreal baroque decor, then slip down to the basement for live music from emerging Milanese talent. If you get hungry, the speciality of the house is Abruzzi-style roast-meat skewers. (www.sacrestia.com; Via Conchetta 20; cocktails €6-8; ⏰6pm-2am; 🚊3, 9)

Surfer's Den

BAR

17 Map p94, D5

This eccentric tiki bar is located in the midst of an ugly sports centre, Centro Sportivo Savorelli. The upside is a nice outdoor garden, a fully equipped barbe-cue grill, deckchairs and DJ sets. If you concentrate on the jaunty umbrella in your cocktail and the strings of party lights, you can almost imagine you're at the beach. (Piazza Caduti del Lavoro 5; ⏰5pm-3am Mon, 7pm-2am Tue-Sat; 🚊15)

La Vineria

WINE BAR

18 Map p94, A3

La Vineria strips away all the *aperitivo* hoopla and serves up glasses, carafes and bottles of wine (and olive oil) straight from the barrel. A glass of wine will set you back just €2 instead of the usual €8. If you do fancy a bite to eat the staff will happily put together a hearty cheese and meat board (€5 to €7). (📞02 8324 2440; www.la-vineria.it; Via Casale 4; ⏰10.30-1.30am Mon-Sat, 4pm-midnight Sun; Porta Genova)

Entertainment

Auditorium di Milano

CLASSICAL MUSIC

19 Map p94, C4

Classical concerts are held at the Auditorium di Milano. (📞02 8338 9422; www.auditoriumdimilano.org; Largo Gustav Mahler; ⏰box office 2.30-7pm Tue-Sun; 🚊3, 9)

Scimmie

LIVE MUSIC

20 Map p94, B4

Jazz, alternative rock and blues are the stock in trade of the emerging talents who play to overflowing crowds inside, outside in the garden and on

CRISTINA FUMI / ALAMY ©

Scimmie

its summertime jazz barge. Concerts start at 10pm. (www.scimmie.it; Via Cardinale Ascanio Sforza 49; admission €10; ⏰8pm-3am Tue-Sat; Ⓜ Porta Genova)

Nibada Theatre LIVE MUSIC

21 ⭐ Map p94, B4

This tiny, unpretentious venue down the heavily graffitied Via Gola has an outsized reputation for hosting stellar live-music performances for serious blues, soul, folk and rock-and-roll bands. Even better, admission is (amazingly) free – if you can squeeze in. (www.nibada.it; Via Gola 12; ⏰from 10.30pm; 🚊3)

Le Trottoir CABARET, LIVE MUSIC

22 ⭐ Map p94, C3

Legendary Le Trottoir is housed in an ex-customs toll gate on the Darsena docks and is a good place to move on to after drinks in Navigli. Cultural events, live music and cabaret are hosted here. Drink upstairs in the psychedelic yellow, blue and red Andrea Pinketts lounge or roll out onto the pavement with hundreds of other revellers in summer. (📞02 837 81 66; www.letrottoir.it; Piazza XXIV Maggio 1; admission €10; ⏰11pm-2am; 🚊3, 9)

Understand

Living by Design

From the cup that holds your morning espresso to the bedside light you click off before you go to sleep, there's a designer responsible – and almost everyone in Milan knows their name.

Design Roots

The roots of Italian design can be found in 1930s Milan with the opening of the Triennale and the development of the Fiera as a modern marketplace. As large-scale industrial design came late to Italy, a decorative joy persisted in production, despite the onslaught of modernist rigour.

Philosopher-Architects

With the end of WWII, the Milanese authorities were preoccupied with rebuilding the bomb-damaged city. Luckily for them the 1930s and '40s spawned a generation of architect-philosophers (Giò Ponti, Piero Fornasetti, Enzo Mari, the Castiglioni brothers, Mario Bellini, Gae Aulenti and Ettore Sottsass). Imbued with modernist optimism, they believed designers and architects' purpose should be to create not only functional objects and spaces, but beautiful ones too.

From Producer...

Milan's designers also benefitted from a unique proximity to a highly skilled artisanal workforce spread across the northern Lombard district of Brianza. Populated by many small craft businesses engaged in textiles (the silk mills of Como), carpentry (the production of furniture and musical instruments), leatherwork and metalwork, Brianza provided a technical workforce that could make modernist dreams come true.

...To Market

While Brianza's production houses remained true to the craft aspect of their work, they were able to move towards modern sales and production techniques via Milan's Fiera. With the opening of the trade Triennale in 1933, Milan established a forum for designers, architects and manufacturers to come together. This connection between producer and marketplace established a happy symbiosis between creativity and commercialism that ultimately fine-tuned Italian design to achieve the modernist ideal of creating desirable, useful objects.

Shopping

Mauro Leone
SHOES

🔒 Map p94, C2

irm favourite with fashionistas on
udget, Mauro Leone's handmade-
Italy footwear offers style for
tween €50 and €80 per pair. Pick
m a range that spans midheeled
kle boots in cobalt blue to ballerina
mps in Ferrari red with a peak of
cleavage; it's no wonder Milanese
e Mauro's shoes. (✆02 5810 5041;
w.mauroleone.com; Corso di Porta Ticinese
; ⏰3-7.30pm Mon, 10am-7.30pm Tue-Sat;
2, 9)

vio
FASHION

🔒 Map p94, C1

e brainchild of San Franciscan
ary Belle Walker, Bivio is a buy-
-trade store offering top quality
e-owned' fashion at a fraction of
original retail price. Eagle-eyed
ary ensures the store is stocked
h the latest trends and colours for
loyal buyers, while traders happily
arge the proceeds of their sales on
ething else. This being Milan, you
bet on some fabulous bargains.
(✆02 5810 8691; www.biviomilano.it; Via
Mora 4; ⏰11am-7.30pm Tue-Sun; 🚊2, 14)

Contrasto Galleria
ARTS

25 🔒 Map p94, C3

This is probably Milan's leading
commercial photographic gallery. It
showcases the work of internationally
famous photographers such as Wil-
liam Klein and Erwin Olaf alongside
intriguing vintage prints and the
work of emerging artists, many of
them Italian. Prices are surprisingly
accessible for lesser-known names.
(✆02 8907 5420; www.contrastogalleria.
com; Via Ascanio Sforza 29; ⏰3-7pm Tue-
Sat; 🚊3, 9)

Biffi
FASHION

26 🔒 Map p94, B1

Retailer Rosy Biffi spotted potential in
the young Giorgio Armani and Gianni
Versace long before they became
household names. More recently, Biffi
got Milanese women hooked onto US
cult-brand jeans. She has a knack for
interpreting edgier trends and making them work for conformist Milan;
check out her selection of international fashion heavyweights for both men
and women. (✆02 831 16 01; www.biffi.
com; Corso Genova 5 & 6; ⏰3-7.30pm Mon,
9.30am-1.30pm & 3-7.30pm Tue-Sat; 🚊2, 14)

Local Life
Porta Romana

The district of Porta Romana runs southeast from the centre and beneath one of the city gates originally built by Barbarossa on the ancient road to Rome in the 12th century. The tree-lined streets are filled with grand *palazzi* (mansions) and good-value dining and drinking options that cater to hospital staff at the Policlinico and students from the Università Statale and Bocconi, Milan's main business school.

Getting There

M **Metro** Porta Romana is accessible on the M3 (yellow line), stopping at Porta Romana and Lodi.

🚊 **Tram** East–west tram 9 connects at Porta Romana.

❶ Fondazione Prada

As creative as the minds that gave it shape, the new **Fondazione Prada** (☎02 5666 2612; www.fondazioneprada. org; Largo Isarco 2; adult/reduced €10/8; ☯10am-9pm; Ⓜ Lodi) has transformed a dilapidated brandy factory into 19,000 sq metres of exciting, multilevel exhibition space. Almost as popular as the exhibits is the Wes Anderson–designed cafe, Bar Luce, with its 1950s-inspired interior.

❷ Cascina Cuccagna

A farmhouse dating from 1695, Cascina Cuccagna has been resurrected as a community hub, hostel and all-day cafe-restaurant. At weekends farmers turn up here with their produce and families come in droves to sit in the pretty garden and scoff locally sourced, organic grub at **Un Posto a Milano** (☎02 545 77 85; www.unpostoamilano.it; Via Cuccagna 2; meals €10-35; ☯12.30-3pm & 7.20-11pm Tue-Sun; ❖❖; Ⓜ Porta Romana).

❸ Sweet Treats

Named after the natural yeast base used by pastry chefs for more than a century, **Pastamadre** (☎02 5519 0020; Via Bernardino Corio 8; meals €25-35; ☯noon-3pm & 7-11pm Mon-Sat; Ⓜ Porta Romana) serves organic breads, croissants and puff pastries stuffed with strawberry frangipane.

❹ Spa Days

Pad down the high hallways of Milan's former public-transport headquarters and make yourself comfortable in a pine-clad railway carriage for a bio sauna session. Such is the ingenuity of the **QC Terme spa** (☎02 5519 9367; www.termemilano. com; Piazzale Medaglie d'Oro 2; day ticket weekdays/weekend €45/50, beauty ticket weekdays/weekend €55/60; ☯9.30am-11pm Mon-Thu & Sun, 8.30-12.30am Fri & Sat; Ⓜ Porta Romana).

❺ Creative Kids Stuff

With its urban bustle and grey skies, Milan might not seem like a child-friendly destination. But the Milanese have kids too, and insist that their children's pleasures are as cool and creative as theirs. Check out the new interactive kids museum **MUBA** (☎02 4398 0402; www.muba.it; Via Enrico Besana 12; child/adult/family €8/6/25; ☯9.30am-3.30pm Mon, to 6.30pm Tue-Fri, 10am-7pm Sat & Sun; ❖; ☒9).

❻ Home Cooking

Judging by the red-and-white checked curtains hanging at the windows and the textbook trattoria interiors, you may fear **La Bettola di Piero** (Via Orti 17; meals €35-45; ☯7pm-midnight Mon, noon-3pm & 7pm-midnight Tue-Sat; Ⓜ Crocetta) is a stereotype too far. That is until you sample the home cooking: wild *puntarelle* (chicory) with an anchovy sauce, bold yellow goose eggs with asparagus, and duck soused in figs and balsamic. Against your will you'll find yourself exclaiming, 'It's just like Nonna used to make!'

Explore

Lago Maggiore & Around

More than its neighbours, lakes Como and Garda, Lago Maggiore has retained the belle époque air of its early tourist heyday, when Napoleon ordered the building of the Simplon Pass through the Alps to Switzerland. Attracted by the mild climate and easy access, the European *haute bourgeoisie* flocked to buy and build grand lakeside villas and established a series of extraordinary gardens around the lake's shore.

The Sights in a Day

☼ Toss a coin to determine which palace to start the day with: for romance and intimate family details opt for **Palazzo Madre** (p107); for art and ostentation head to **Palazzo Borromeo** (p107), where Prince Charles and Princess Diana holidayed in 1985 as the guests of the Borromei family.

☀ For lunch make sure you've booked in for fine lakeside dining at **Ristorante Milano** (p111) or **Il Vicoletto** (p110), where you should order Lago Maggiore's speciality trout or char and a bottle of wine from nearby Franciacorte vineyards.

☾ After lunch plan on taking it easy with an amble through the tropical hothouses and camellia groves of **Villa Taranto** (p111) in Verbania. Then walk back to Verbania Intra via the lakeside path for *aperitivo* (see p97) at **La Bottiglieria** (p111) or head back to Stresa for movie-star cocktails on the terrace at the **Grand Hotel des Iles Borromées** (p111).

◉ Top Sights

Isole Borromee (p106)

♥ Best of the Lakes

History

Isole Borromee (p106)

Santa Caterina del Sasso (p112)

Basilica di San Giulio (p113)

Gardens

Villa Taranto (p111)

Palazzo Borromeo (p107)

Palazzo Madre (p107)

Eating

Ristorante Milano (p111)

Locanda di Orta (p113)

Drinking

Grand Hotel des Iles Borromées (p111)

Getting There

🚃 **Train** Stresa is on the Milan–Domodossola line. Trains leave Milan's Stazione Centrale hourly.

⛴ **Boat** Navigazione Lago Maggiore (p110) operates ferries and hydrofoils on Lago Maggiore. Ticket booths are next to the embarkation quays. Navigazione Lago d'Orta (p112) operates ferries on Lago d'Orta from Orta San Giulio.

Top Sights
Isole Borromee

The Borromean Gulf forms Lago Maggiore's most beautiful corner, and the Isole Borromee (Borromean Islands) harbour its most spectacular sights: the privately owned palaces of the Borromei family. Closest to Stresa is Isola Bella with its ostentatious terraces and cool shell-encrusted grottoes, while the luxuriant tropical gardens of Isola Madre beckon further afield. Sharing the gulf is modest Isola Superiore (Fisherman's Island). It has no palaces, but its narrow cobbled streets, pretty harbour and first-class restaurants make it an enchanting stop.

☏ 0323 3 05 56

www.borromeoturismo.it

combined ticket adult/child €21/10

🕙 9am-5.30pm mid-Mar–mid-Oct

Italian Garden, Isola Bella

Don't Miss

Palazzo Borromeo

Isola Bella took the name of Carlo III's wife, the *bella* Isabella, in the 17th century when its centre-piece, **Palazzo Borromeo** (adult/child €15/8.50, incl Palazzo Madre adult/child €21/10), was built. Presiding over 10 tiers of spectacular terraced gardens, this baroque palace is Lago Maggiore's finest building. Wandering the sumptuous interiors reveals guest rooms, studies and reception halls. Particularly striking are the Sala di Napoleone, where the emperor Napoleon stayed with his wife in 1797; the Sala da Ballo (Ballroom); the ornate Sala del Trono (Throne Room); and the Sala delle Regine (Queen's Room). Paintings from a 130-strong Borromeo collection hang all around.

Palazzo Madre

The fabulous **Palazzo Madre** (adult/child €12/6.50, incl Palazzo Borromeo €21/10) *is* the island of Madre. White peacocks with bristling feathers resembling bridal gowns strut around English-style gardens ablaze with azaleas, rhododendrons, camellias and hibiscus. Inside the 16th- to 18th-century palace you'll find the Countess Borromeo's doll collection, a neoclassical puppet theatre designed by a scenographer from Milan's Teatro alla Scala (La Scala), and a 'horror' theatre with a cast of devilish marionettes.

Isola Superiore

Lacking any specific sights, tiny 'Fishermen's Island' retains much of its original village atmosphere. A huddle of streets shelters the **Chiesa di San Vittore**, which features an 11th-century apse and a 16th-century fresco. But the real reason to visit is the island's restaurants, which specialise in grilled fish.

☑ Top Tips

▶ Give yourself at least half a day to enjoy each palace.

▶ The Palazzo Borromeo's fine art collection includes Old Master works by Rubens, Titian, Andrea Mantegna and Antonio Canova.

▶ Don't miss the 3000-year-old fossilised boat displayed in the grotto of Palazzo Borromeo.

✗ Take a Break

There is only one cafe on Isola Madre, serving drinks and small snacks, and one restaurant on Isola Bella, **Elvezia** (☏ 0323 3 00 43; Via Vittorio Emanuele 18; meals €30-35; ⏰ noon-2pm & 6.30-9pm Tue-Sun Mar-Oct, Fri-Sun only Nov-Feb).

For lunch, head over to Isola Superiore for an excellent seafood lunch at **Casabella** (☏ 0323 3 34 71; www.isola-pescatori.it; Via del Marinaio 1; meals €30-50, 5-course tasting menu €55; ⏰ noon-2pm & 6-8.30pm Feb-Nov).

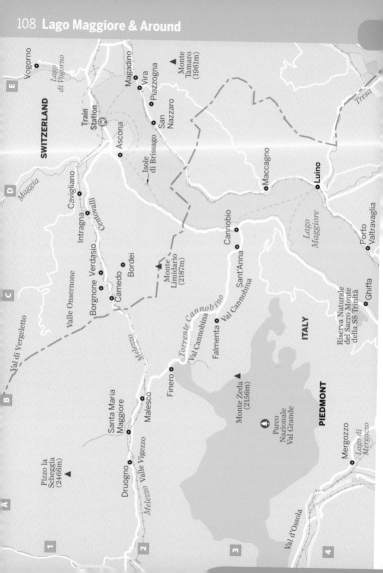

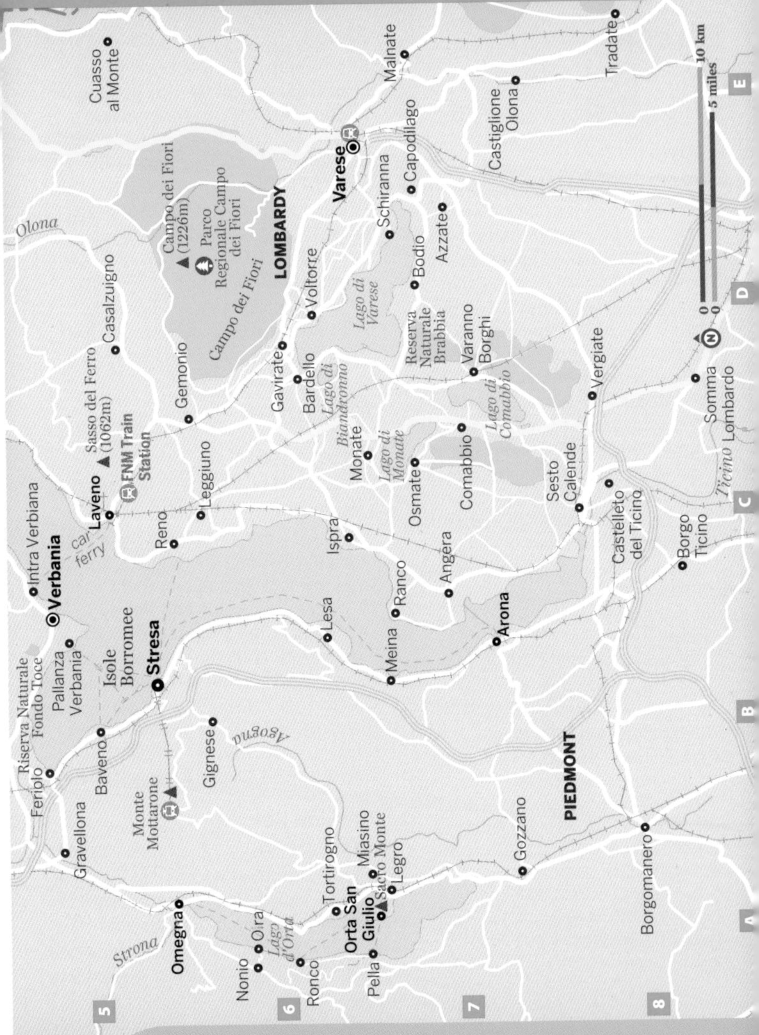

Cuasso al Monte

Malnate

Tradate

Castiglione Olona

Varese

Capodilago

10 km

5 miles

Olona

Campo dei Fiori (1226m)

Parco Regionale Campo dei Fiori

LOMBARDY

Schiranna

Voltorre

Bodio

Azzate

Casalzuigno

Gemonio

Gaviate

Bardello

Lago di Biandronno

Lago di Varese

Reserva Naturale Brabbia

Varanno

Borghi

Lago di Comabbio

Vergiate

Somma Lombardo

Sasso del Ferro (1062m)

FNM Train Station

Leggiuno

Monate

Lago di Monate

Osmate

Comabbio

Sesto Calende

Castelleto del Ticino

Ticino

Intra Verbiana

Laveno

Reno

Ispra

Angera

Arona

Borgo Ticino

car ferry

Verbania

Lesa

Ranco

Reserva Naturale Fondo Toce

Pallanza Verbania

Isole Borromee

Stresa

Meina

Feriolo

Baveno

Gignese

Aveno

Monte Mottarone

Gozzano

PIEDMONT

Gravellona

Tortirogno

Miasino

Sacro Monte

Orta San Giulio

Legro

Borgomanero

Ora

Lago d'Orta

Omegna

Nonio

Ronco

Pella

Strona

Stresa

MAP P108, B5

⊙ Sights

Funivia Stresa–Mottarone
CABLE CAR

Captivating lake views unfold during a 20-minute cable-car journey to the top of 1491m-high Monte Mottarone. On a clear day you can see Lago Maggiore, Lago d'Orta and Monte Rosa, on the Swiss border. At the **Alpino** midstation a profusion of Alpine plants flourish in the **Giardino Botanico Alpinia** (✆0323 3 02 95; adult/reduced €3/2.50; ⊙9.30am-6pm Apr-Oct). The mountain itself offers good hiking and biking trails. At time of writing the cable car was closed for repairs; a reopening date hadn't been set. (✆0323 3 02 95; www.stresa-mottarone.it; Piazzale della Funivia; return adult/reduced €13.50/8.50, to Alpino station €8/5.50; ⊙9.30am-5.30pm Apr-Oct, 8.10am-5.30pm Nov-Mar)

✅ Top Tip

Ferries on Lago Maggiore

Navigazione Lago Maggiore
(✆800 551801; www.navigazionelaghi.it) boat services include those connecting Stresa with Arona (€6.20, 40 minutes) and Verbania Pallanza (often just called Pallanza; €5, 35 minutes). Day passes include a ticket linking Stresa with Isola Superiore, Isola Bella and Isola Madre (€16.90). Services are reduced in autumn and winter.

Bicicò
MOUNTAIN BIKING

Bicicò rents mountain bikes from its base at the foot of the Stresa–Monte Mottarone cable car. Rates include a helmet and road book detailing an easy 25km, three-hour panoramic descent from the mountain top back to Stresa. Also runs guided trips (half-/full day €80/150) and advises on other mountain- and road-bike routes. Book trips and hire two days in advance. (✆340 3572189; www.bicico.it; Piazzale della Funivia; half-/full-day rental €25/30; ⊙9.30am-12.30pm & 1.30-5.30pm)

⊗ Eating

Ristorante Il Vicoletto
RISTORANTE €€

Located a short, uphill walk from the centre of Stresa, Il Vicoletto has a commendable regional menu including lake trout, wild asparagus, and traditional risotto with radicchio and Taleggio cheese. The dining room is modestly elegant with bottle-lined dressers and linen-covered tables, while the local clientele speaks volumes in this tourist town. (✆0323 93 21 02; www.ristorantevicoletto.com; Vicolo del Pocivo 3; meals €30-45; ⊙noon-2pm & 6.30-10pm Fri-Wed)

Taverna del Pappagallo
TRATTORIA €

It's not fancy and it's not superserious, but this welcoming backstreet trattoria is where you'll find Stresa's families tucking into tasty regional dishes ranging from pizzas cooked in an old wood-fired oven to risotto with lake fish. (📞0323 3 04 11; www.tavernapappagallo.com; Via Principessa Margherita 46; meals €20-25; ⏰6.30-11pm Thu-Tue)

🍷 Drinking

Grand Hotel des Iles Borromées
COCKTAIL BAR

Following his WWI stint on the Italian front, Ernest Hemingway checked in here to nurse his battle scars and to write *A Farewell to Arms*. The passionate antiwar novel featured this sumptuous hotel. You might baulk at room prices but you can still slug back a manhattan on the terraces with cinematic views. (📞0323 93 89 38; www.borromees.it; Corso Umberto I 67; ⏰6pm-late)

Verbania

MAP P108, B5

🎯 Sights

Villa Taranto
GARDENS

The grounds of this late-19th-century villa are one of Lago Maggiore's highlights. A Scottish captain, Neil McEacharn, bought the Normandy-style villa from the Savoy family in 1931 after spotting an ad in the *Times*. He planted some 20,000 plant species over 30 years, and today it's considered one of Europe's finest botanic gardens. Even the main entrance path is a grand affair,

bordered by lawns and a cornucopia of colourful flowers. It's a short walk from the Villa Taranto ferry stop. (📞0323 55 66 67; www.villataranto.it; Via Vittorio Veneto 111, Verbania Pallanza; adult/reduced €10/5.50; ⏰8.30am-6.30pm mid-Mar–Sep, 9am-4pm Oct; P)

🍴 Eating

Ristorante Milano
MODERN ITALIAN €€€

The setting really is hard to beat: Milano directly overlooks Pallanza's minuscule horseshoe-shaped harbour (200m south of the ferry jetty); a scattering of tables sits on lakeside lawns amid the trees. It's an idyllic spot to enjoy lake fish, local lamb and some innovative Italian cuisine, such as *risotto ai petali di rosa* (risotto with rose petals). (📞0323 55 68 16; www.ristorantemilanolagomaggiore.it; Corso Zanitello 2, Verbania Pallanza; meals €50-70; ⏰noon-2pm & 7-9pm Wed-Sun, noon-2pm Mon; ❄)

🍷 Drinking

La Bottiglieria del Castello
WINE BAR

Sample mountain cheeses with a glass of Dolcetto in the pretty piazza at Intra Verbania. If you do you'll be upholding a proud tradition, started in 1905 when sister restaurant **Osteria Castello** (📞0323 51 65 79; www.osteriacastello.com; Piazza Castello 9, Verbania Intra; meals €25; ⏰11am-3pm & 6pm-midnight, closed Sun), just next door, served tumblers of wine to mill workers and fishers who came here to drink and catch up on the daily news. (☎0323 51 65 79; www.osteriacastello.com; Piazza Castello 5, Verbania Intra; ⏱11am-3pm & 6-9pm Mon-Sat)

Santa Caterina del Sasso

MAP P108, C6

Sights

Santa Caterina del Sasso
MONASTERY

One of northern Italy's most spectacularly sited monasteries, Santa Caterina del Sasso clings to the high rocky face of Lago Maggiore's southeast shore. The buildings span the 13th and 14th centuries; the porticoes and chapels are packed with frescoes; and the views from the tiny courtyards are superb. The monastery is reached either by climbing up 80 steps from

Top Tip

Ferries on Lago d'Orta

Navigazione Lago d'Orta (☎345 517 00 05; www.navigazionelagodorta. it) boats depart from the landing stage on Piazza Motta in Orta San Giulio to Isola San Giulio (one-way/ return €2/3). A day ticket for unlimited travel anywhere on the lake costs €8.

the Santa Caterina ferry quay, or by clattering down a 268-step staircase from the car park (there is a lift too). (www.santacaterinadelsasso.com; Via Santa Caterina 13; admission free; ⏱9am-noon & 2-6pm Apr-Sep, to 5pm Mar & Oct, closed weekdays Nov-Feb)

Arona

MAP P108, B7

Sights

Sacro Monte di San Carlo
LANDMARK

When Milan's superstar bishop San Carlo Borromeo (1538–84) was declared a saint in 1610, his cousin, Federico, ordered the creation of a *sacro monte* in his memory, featuring 15 chapels lining a path to a church. The church and three of those chapels were built, along with a special extra: a hollow 35m bronze-and-copper statue of the saint. It's commonly known as the Sancarlone (Big St Charles), and you can climb up inside it to discover spectacular views through the giant's eyes. (☎0322 24 96 69; Piazza San Carlo; admission €7; ⏱9am-12.30pm & 2.30-6pm Apr-Oct, to 4.30pm Sat & Sun Nov-Mar)

✕ Eating

Taverna del Pittore
RISTORANTE €€€

What is possibly Lago Maggiore's most romantic restaurant has a waterside terrace and views of the illuminated

Rocca di Angera fortress at night. The refined food is no less fabulous, with squid, duck and octopus transformed into exquisitely arranged dishes featuring ravioli, broth, risotto and gnocchi. (☏0322 24 33 66; www.ristorantetavernadelpittore.it; Piazza del Popolo 39; meals €60-80; ☺noon-2.30pm & 7.30-10pm Fri-Wed; ❄)

Lago d'Orta

MAP P108, A6

Sights

Orta San Giulio Old Town
VILLAGE

The medieval village of Orta San Giulio (population just 1150), often referred to simply as Orta, is the focal point of Lago d'Orta and is the lake's main village. At its heart, the central square, Piazza Motta, is framed by cream-coloured houses roofed with thick slate tiles. It's overlooked by the Palazotto, a frescoed 16th-century building borne up by stilts above a small loggia.

Basilica di San Giulio
CHURCH

Isola San Giulio is dominated at its south end by the 12th-century Basilica di San Giulio, which is full of vibrant frescoes that alone make a trip to the island worthwhile. The church, island and mainland town are named after a Greek evangelist, Giulio, who's said to have rid the island of snakes, dragons and assorted monsters in the late 4th century. Regular ferries shuttle between the island and Orta San Giulio (☺9.30am-6pm Tue-Sun, 2-5pm Mon Apr-Sep, 9.30am-noon & 2-5pm Tue-Sun, 2-5pm Mon Oct-Mar)

✖ Eating

Locanda di Orta
MODERN ITALIAN €€€

Tiny Orta can now boast its very own Michelin star – in the wisteria-draped Locanda di Orta, squeezed into the heart of the old town. It's a supremely stylish, intimate affair (it only seats around 17 people) where culinary alchemy converts traditional Lago d'Orta ingredients into works of foodie art. (☏0322 90 51 88; www.locandaorta.com; Via Olina 18, Orta San Giulio; meals €50; ☺noon-2.30pm & 7.30-9pm)

Venus
TRATTORIA €€

The place with the best views is also one of the best places to eat in town. The menu of rich local dishes might feature a creamy risotto flavoured with cheese, venison and blueberries, or polenta with cheese, cabbage and pistachios. (☏0322 9 03 62; www.venusorta.it; Piazza Motta 50, Orta San Giulio; meals €20-30; ☺noon-3pm & 6-10pm Tue-Sun)

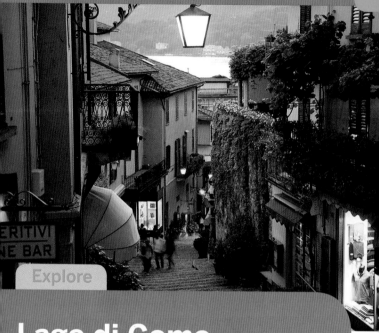

Explore

Lago di Como & Around

Set in the shadow of the snow-covered Rhaetian Alps and hemmed in by steep, wooded hills, Lago di Como (also known as Lago di Lario) is the most spectacular of the northern Italian lakes. Shaped like an upside-down letter Y, its winding shoreline is scattered with villages, including delightful Bellagio, which sits at the centre of the two southern branches on a small promontory.

The Sights in a Day

☀ For optimum access to all the lake sites, situate yourself in **Bellagio** (p116). Here your morning coffee run may involve a walk through the elegant lakeside gardens of **Villa Melzi** (p117) to Piazza Mazzini, where you can board the hydrofoil for the sculptures in Tremezzo's **Villa Carlotta** (p124) or the spectacular gardens of **Villa Balbianello** (p123).

☀ In Como take the pleasant lake-front stroll, **Passeggiata Lino Gelpi** (p120), past waterfront mansions to arrive on the doorstep of **Villa Olmo** (p120), where you can wander the gardens, enjoy world-class art or laze around the scenic **lido** (p121).

☾ For sunset take a seaplane from **Aero Club Como** (p122) over the lake or head up to Brunate in the **cable car** (p122) for panoramic views. Then for dinner, reserve a table in Bellagio at **Hotel Silvio** (p117) or in Como at **Osteria del Gallo** (p122) for classic lakeside fare. Or, for a bit of movie-star magic, taxi up to the terrace of **Il Gatto Nero** (p125) above Cernobbio and watch the lights on the lake twinkle like stars.

◉ Top Sights
Bellagio (p116)

❤ Best of the Lakes

Gardens

Villa del Balbianello (p123)

Villa Melzi d'Eril (p117)

Villa Monastero (p124)

Eating

Il Gatto Nero (p125)

Osteria del Gallo (p122)

Vecchia Varenna (p125)

Lake Experiences

Aero Club Como (p122)

Lido Villa Olmo (p121)

Barindelli's (p117)

Getting There

🚄 **Train** From Milan's Stazione Centrale and Porta Garibaldi hourly services run to Como San Giovanni station. Trains from Milan's Stazione Nord arrive at Como's lakeside Stazione FNM (listed on time-tables as Como Nord Lago).

⚓ **Boat** Navigazione Lago di Como (p122) operates ferries and hydrofoils around the lake. Ticket booths are located next to the embarkation quay.

Top Sights
Bellagio

It's impossible not to be charmed by Bellagio's waterfront of bobbing boats, its maze of steep stone staircases, its dark cypress groves and the showy rhododendron-filled gardens. Its peerless position on the promontory jutting out into the centre of the lake made it the object of much squabbling between Milan and Como, hence its ruined fortifications and its church of San Giovanni, built by Como masters between 1075 and 1125. Although it teems with visitors in summer, if you turn up out of season, you'll have the place almost to yourself.

◉ Map p118, D5

www.bellagiolakecomo.com

Bellagio, Lago di Como

Don't Miss

Villa Serbelloni

Bellagio has been a favoured summer resort since Roman times, when Pliny the Younger holidayed on the promontory where **Villa Serbelloni** (📞031 95 15 55; Piazza della Chiesa 14; adult/child €9/5; ⏰tours 11.30am & 2.30pm Tue-Sun mid-Mar–Oct) now stands. The Romans introduced the olive and laurel trees that dot the 20-hectare gardens, which took on their Italianate, English and Mediterranean designs at the beginning of the 19th century. The villa, now privately owned by the Rockefeller Foundation, still hosts scholars and academics but the gardens with their unique views are open for tours.

Villa Melzi d'Eril

Built in 1808 for Francesco Melzi d'Eril (1753–1816), Napoleon's advisor and vice president of the First Italian Republic, **Villa Melzi** (📞339 4573838; www.giardinidivillamelzi.it; Lungo Lario Manzoni; adult/reduced €6.50/4; ⏰9.30am-6.30pm Apr-Oct) is one of the most elegant villas on the lake. The neoclassical temple is where Liszt came over all romantic and composed his 1837 sonata dedicated to Dante and Beatrice.

Lake Tours

For a touch of Clooney-esque glamour, consider taking a tour of the lake in one of **Barindelli's** (📞338 2110337; www.barindellitaxiboats.it; Piazza Mazzini; tours per hour €140) slick mahogany cigarette boats. Hour-long sunset tours (€140 for up to 12 people) take you around Bellagio's headland, where you can view the splendour of Villa Serbelloni from the water. Alternatively, DIY it on a kayak tour with **Bellagio Water Sports** (📞340 3949375; www.bellagiowatersports.com; Pescallo Harbour; rental per 2/4hr €18/30, tours €35), an experienced outfit in Pescallo, on the east side of the Bellagio headland.

☑ Top Tips

▶ The gardens are at their finest between March and May, when the camellias, azaleas, orchids and rhododendrons bloom.

▶ Book guided tours of Villa Serbelloni's gardens with **PromoBellagio** (Map p118, D5; Piazza della Chiesa 14; ⏰9.30am-1pm Mon, 9-11am & 1.30-3.30pm Tue-Sun Apr-Oct).

▶ Bellagio's new **Lido** (www.lidodibellagio.com; Via Carcano 1; per half-/full day €8/12; ⏰10.30am-6.30pm Tue-Sun May, Jun & Sep, daily to 7.30pm Jul & Aug) comes with sand-scattered decking and diving platforms over the lake.

✕ Take a Break

Break for a cappuccino at historic **Bar Rossi** (📞031 95 01 96; Piazza Mazzini 22; snacks €3-8; ⏰7.30am-midnight Apr-Sep, to 10.30pm Oct-Mar).

For lunch, dine on the terrace at **Hotel Silvio** (📞031 95 03 22; www.bellagiosilvio.com; Via Carcano 10; meals €30-40; 🅿✳🛜).

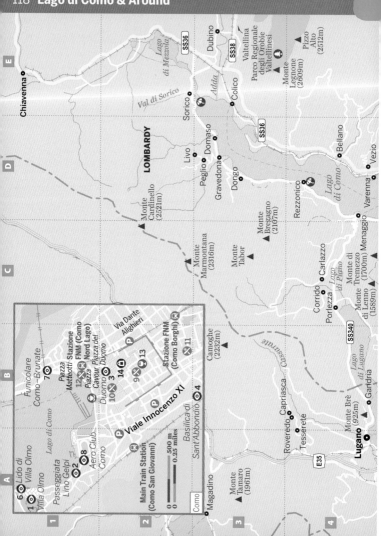

Chiavenna

Lago di Mezzola

SS36

Dubino

SS38

Valtellina
Parco Regionale
degli Orobie
Valtellinesi

Pizzo
Alto
(2512m)

Monte
Legnone
(2609m)

Val di Sorico

Adda

Sorico

Colico

LOMBARDY

Livo

Peglio

Domaso

Gravedona

Dongo

SS36

Bellano

Vezio

Lago
di Como

Varenna

Rezzonico

Monte
Cardinello
(2521m)

Monte
Bregagno
(2107m)

Monte
Marmontana
(2316m)

Monte
Tabor

Corrido

Carlazzo

Lago
di Piano

Porlezza

Monte di
Tremezzo
(1700m)

Monte di
Lenno
(1589m)

Menaggio

SS340

Cressarate

Camoghe
(2232m)

Lago
di Lugano

SS340

E35

Capriasca

Roveredo

Tesserete

Gandria

Monte Brè
(925m)

Lugano

Funicolare
Como–Brunate

Piazza
Matteotti

Stazione
FNM (Como
Nord Lago)

Via Dante
Alighieri

Stazione FNM
(Como Borghi)

Piazza
Cavour

Piazza del
Duomo

Piazza
Duomo

Lago di Como

Passeggiata
Lino Gelpi

Aero Club
Como

Viale Innocenzo XI

Basilica di
Sant'Abbondio

Main Train Station
(Como San Giovanni)

Lido di
Villa Olmo

Villa Olmo

Magadino

Monte
Tamaro
(1961m)

Como

0   500 m
0   0.25 miles

Piani di Bobbio

Enna

SP62

Ballabio Superiore

La Grigna Settentrionale (2408m) ▲

SP65

Pioverna

Laorca

◉ **Lecco**

SS36

Lago di Garlate

Civate

Lago di Annone Garlate

Lago di Olginate

Oggiono

SS36

10 km
5 miles

N ↑

Cadenabbia

Punta Spartivento

⊗17 ◉16 **Bellagio**
Tremezzo ⊗ Villa ⊕ ⊕ Promo Bellagio
Lenno • Carlotta Loppia SP2
Isola 15 ⊕ Villa Balbianello
Comacina

SS583 Monte San Primo (1685m) ▲

Malgrate

Maggreglio ▲
Onno
Barni
Lezzeno

SS36

Magreglio
Onno Lasnigo

Nesso
Careno Triangolo Lariano Sormano
Argegno Pognana Lario
Lario

LOMBARDY

Lago di Segrino

Lago di Pusiano

Erba •

Lago di Alserio

SP13

SS340

Laglio

Monte Bishino (1325m) ▲
Tosnacco
Torno

ITALY

Brunate

◉ **Como** 5 ⊕ Museo della Seta

Lago di Montorfano

Cantù •

SS342

Blevio

Monte Generoso (1701m) ▲

Campione d'Italia

Breggia

Cernobbio

Mendrisio

E35

Chiasso

See Como Enlargement

SS35

E35

San Salvatore (912m) ▲

Mara

Parco Botanico San Grato
Monte Arbostora (822m) ▲
Monte San Giorgio (1090m) ▲

Viggiù

Malnate

Solbiate

Olgiate Caccivio
Olgiate Comasco

Parco Regionale del Pineta di Apianö ▲

Mozzate •

SS344

SP242

Cuasso al Monte

Tradate •

SP42

Como

Villa Olmo

HISTORIC BUILDING

1 ◎ Map p118, A1

Set facing the lake, the grand creamy facade of neoclassical Villa Olmo is one of Como's biggest landmarks. The extravagant structure was built in 1728 by the Odescalchi family, related to Pope Innocent XI. If there's an art exhibition showing, you'll get to admire the sumptuous Liberty-style interiors. Otherwise, you can enjoy the Italianate and English gardens. (☎031 25 23 52; Via Cantoni 1; gardens free, villa entry varies by exhibition; ☉villa during exhibitions 9am-12.30pm & 2-5pm Mon-Sat, gardens 7.30am-11pm summer, to 7pm winter)

Local Life
Clooney's Como

Sample the film-star lifestyle by doing Lago di Como Clooney-style: slug back a cocktail at **Harry's Bar** (Map p118, B6; Piazza Risorgimento 2; ☉10am-midnight), Clooney's local in Cernobbio; travel by motorbike amid Como's hills with **Lake Como Motorbike** (☎349 4277542; www.lakecomomotorbike.com); or book a cigarette boat with Barindelli's (p117) for a cinematic trip. Afterwards, drop by Il Gatto Nero (p125) for dinner, just as the films stars do...

Passeggiata Lino Gelpi

WATERFRONT

2 ◎ Map p118, A1

One of Como's most charming walks is the lakeside stroll west from Piazza Cavour. Passeggiata Lino Gelpi leads past the **Monumento ai Caduti** (War Memorial; Viale Puecher 9), a 1931 memorial to Italy's WWI dead and a classic example of Fascist-era architecture. Next you'll pass a series of mansions and villas – including **Villa Saporiti** and **Villa Gallia**, both now owned by the provincial government and closed to the public – before arriving at the garden-ringed Villa Olmo.

Duomo

CATHEDRAL

3 ◎ Map p118, B2

Although largely Gothic in style, elements of Romanesque, Renaissance and baroque can also be seen in Como's imposing, marble-clad *duomo*. The cathedral was built between the 14th and 18th centuries, and is crowned by a high octagonal dome. (Piazza del Duomo; ☉7.30am-7.30pm Mon-Sat, to 9.30pm Sun)

Basilica di Sant'Abbondio

BASILICA

4 ◎ Map p118, B3

About 500m south of the city walls is the remarkable 11th-century Romanesque Basilica di Sant'Abbondio. Aside from its proud, high structure and impressive apse decorated with a

Villa Olmo

beautiful geometric relief around the outside windows, the highlights are the extraordinary frescoes inside the apse. (Via Regina; ☺8am-6pm summer, to 4pm winter)

Museo della Seta   MUSEUM

5 ◉ Map p118, B7

Lago di Como's aspiring silk makers still learn their trade in the 1970s-built Istituto Tecnico Industriale di Setificio textile technical school. It's also home to the Museo della Seta, which draws together the threads of the town's silk history. Early dyeing and printing equipment features amid displays that chart the entire fabric-production process. (Silk Museum; ☎031 30 31 80; www.museosetacomo.com; Via Castelnuovo 9; adult/reduced €10/7; ☺10am-6pm Tue-Fri, to 1pm Sat)

Lido di Villa Olmo   SWIMMING

6 ◉ Map p118, A1

What a delight: a compact *lido* (beach) where you can plunge into open-air pools, sunbathe beside the lake, rent boats, sip cocktails at the waterfront bar and soak up mountain views. Bliss. (☎031 57 08 71; www.lidovillaolmo.it; Via Cernobbio 2; adult/reduced €7/3.50; ☺9am-7pm mid-May–Sep)

Funicolare Como–Brunate

CABLE CAR

7 Map p118, B1

Prepare for some spectacular views. The Como–Brunate cable car (built in 1894) takes seven minutes to trundle up to the quiet hilltop village of **Brunate** (720m), revealing a memorable panorama of mountains and lakes. From there a steep 30-minute walk along a stony mule track leads to **San Maurizio** (907m), where 143 steps climb to the top of a lighthouse. (☑031 30 36 08; www.funicolarecomo.it; Piazza de Gasperi 4; adult one way/return €3/5.50, reduced €2/3.20; ☉half-hourly departures 8am-midnight summer, to 10.30pm winter)

Aero Club Como

SCENIC FLIGHTS

8 Map p118, A1

For a true touch of glamour, take one of these seaplane tours and buzz about the skies high above Como. The often-bumpy take-off and landing on the lake itself is thrilling, as are the views down

Top Tip

Ferries on Lago di Como

Navigazione Lago di Como (☑800 551801; www.navigazionelaghi.it) fast hydrofoils depart from the jetties in Como beside Piazza Cavour. Single fares cost €8.40 to Lenno, €10.40 to Tremezzo, €10.40 to Bellagio and €11.60 to Varenna. Return fares cost double. Zonal passes (per day €6.90 to €28) allow unlimited journeys and can work out cheaper.

onto the miniature villas and villages dotted far below. Flights are popular; in summer book three or four days ahead. (☑031 57 44 95; www.aeroclubcomo. com; Viale Masia 44; 30min flight from €140)

Natta Café

CAFE €

9 Map p118, B2

It's almost as if this is an *osteria* (casual eatery with a host) for the next generation. Yes, there's a proud focus on superb local ingredients and classic wines, but this laid-back cafe also has a beatnik atmosphere. So you get Chianti on the wine list, risotto with lake perch on the menu and Edith Piaf on the sound track. One cool vibe. (☑031 26 91 23; www.nattacafe.com; Via Natta 16; meals €15-20; ☉12.30-3pm & 6.30-midnight Tue-Sat, 12.30-3pm & 7.30-11.30pm Sun; ☎)

Osteria del Gallo

ITALIAN €€

10 Map p118, B2

An ageless *osteria* that looks exactly the part. In the wood-lined dining room, wine bottles and other goodies fill the shelves, and diners sit at small timber tables to tuck into traditional local food. The menu is chalked up daily and might include a first course of *zuppa di ceci* (chickpea soup), followed by lightly fried lake fish. (☑031 27 25 91; www. osteriadelgallo-como.it; Via Vitani 16; meals €25-30; ☉12.30-3pm Mon, to 9pm Tue-Sat)

Enoteca 84

ITALIAN €

11 Map p118, B2

It has the feel of a neighbourhood eatery – and that's because it is.

Set outside Como's pedestrianised core, this snug spot has a handful of traditional dishes on its menu, which might include *lavarello* (white fish) in butter and sage, polenta with beef and mushrooms or *pappardelle alla lepre* (ribbon pasta with hare). (☑031 27 04 82; Via Milano 84; meals €20-25; ☺10am-2.30pm & 7-10pm)

Gelateria Ceccato

GELATERIA €

12 Map p118, B1

For generations *comaschi* (people from Como) have turned to Ceccato for their Sunday-afternoon gelato and then embarked on a ritual *passeggiata* (stroll) with their dripping cones along the lakeshore. You can do no better than imitate them: order a creamy *stracciatella* (chocolate chip) or perhaps a mix of fresh fruit flavours and head off for a relaxed promenade. (☑031 2 33 91; Lungo Lario Trieste 16; gelato €2-4; ☺noon-midnight summer, hours vary winter)

Enoteca Castiglioni

WINE BAR

13 Map p118, B2

If you're lucky you'll bag one of the clutch of tiny tables beside the ranks of wine-bottle lined shelves. It's a smart, modern setting in which to sample top-quality deli produce along with first-rate vintages. (☑031 26 18 60; www.castiglionistore.com; Via Rovelli 17; ☺10am-8pm Mon-Fri, to 9pm Sun)

Top Tip

Visiting Villa Balbianello

Visitors are only permitted to walk the 1km path (amid vegetation so florid as to seem Southeast Asian) from the Lenno landing stage to the Balbianello estate on Tuesdays and at weekends. At other times you have to take a taxi boat from Lenno. If you want to see inside the villa, you must join a guided tour (generally conducted in Italian) by 4.15pm.

A Picci

GIFTS

14 Map p118, B2

First opened in 1919, this is the last remaining silk shop in town dedicated to selling Como-designed-and-made silk ties, scarves, throws and sarongs. Products are grouped in price category (starting at €10 for a tie), reflecting the skill and workmanship involved.

Sales assistants are happy to advise on colours and styles – if it's a gift, they'll also wrap it for you. (☑031 26 13 69; Via Vittorio Emanuele II 54; ☺3-7.30pm Mon, 9am-12.30pm & 3-7.30pm Tue-Sat)

Lenno

Villa Balbianello

HOUSE, GARDENS

15 Map p118, C5

A 1km walk along the lake shore from Lenno's main square, Villa Balbianello has cinematic pedigree: this was where scenes from *Star Wars Episode II* and the 2006 James Bond remake of *Casino Royale* were shot. The reason? It is one of the most dramatic locations anywhere on Lago di Como, providing a genuinely stunning marriage of architecture and lake views. (☑0344 5 61 10; www.fondoambiente.it; Via Comoedia 5, Località Balbianello; villa & gardens adult/reduced €15/7; gardens only adult/reduced €8/3; ☺gardens 10am-6pm Tue & Thu-Sun mid-Mar–mid-Nov)

Tremezzo

MAP P118, C5

Villa Carlotta HOUSE, GARDENS

16 ☉ Map p118, D5

Waterfront Villa Carlotta sits high on Como's must-visit list. The botanic gardens are filled with colour from orange trees interlaced with pergolas, while some of Europe's finest rhododendrons, azaleas and camellias bloom. The 17th-century villa, strung with paintings, sculptures (some by Antonio Canova) and tapestries, takes its name from the Prussian princess who was given the place in 1847 as a wedding present from her mother. (☑0344 404 05; www.villacarlotta.it; Via Regina 2; adult/reduced €9/7; ☺9am-7.30pm Apr–mid-Oct)

Al Veluu RISTORANTE €€€

17 ✗ Map p118, C5

Situated on a steep hillside with panoramic lake views from its

terrace, this excellent restaurant serves up home-cooked dishes that are prepared with great pride. They also reflect Lago di Como's seasonal produce, so expect butter-soft, milk-fed kid with rosemary at Easter or wild asparagus and polenta in spring. (☑0344 4 05 10; www.alveluu.com; Via Rogaro 11; meals €40-70; ☺noon-2.30pm & 7-10pm Wed-Mon; ✦)

Varenna

MAP P118, D4

☉ Sights

Villa Cipressi GARDENS

In Villa Cipressi's gardens cypress trees, palms, magnolias and camellias fill terraces that descend to the lake. Even getting here is picturesque: from the square next to the boat jetty (Piazzale Martiri della Libertà), follow the narrow lakeside promenade around the shore then bear left (inland) up the steps to central Piazza San Giorgio. The villa is signposted from there. (☑0341 83 01 13; www.hotelvillacipressi.it; Via IV Novembre 22; adult/child €4/2; ☺10am-6pm Mar-Oct)

Villa Monastero HOUSE, GARDENS

At Villa Monastero elegant balustrades and statues sit amid exotic shrubs; spiky yucca trees frame lake and mountain views. The villa itself is a former convent that was turned into a private residence in the 18th century – which explains the giddy

opulence of some of the 11 rooms.
(☑0341 29 54 50; www.villamonastero.
eu; Via IV Novembre; villa & gardens adult/
reduced €8/4, gardens only €5/2; ☺gardens
9.30am-7pm, villa 9.30am-7pm Fri-Sun Mar-
Jul & Sep, daily Aug)

Eating

Ristorante La Vista   ITALIAN €€

The fabulous views from the terrace
high in Varenna's old town are only
half the story here. The fresh, inventive food is from a menu that changes
with the seasons; service rarely misses
a beat. (☑0341 83 02 98; www.varenna.
net; Via XX Settembre 35; meals €39-46, 3/4
courses €45/48; ☺7-10pm Wed-Sat & Mon
mid-Mar–late Oct)

Vecchia Varenna   ITALIAN €€

You can't get more lakeside than
these 15 or so tables set on a terrace
suspended over the water. Which
means you can dine on lake fish,
duck breast or little gnocchi cooked
in goat cheese, cream and truffle oil
while gazing over towards Como's
western shore. (☑0341 83 07 93; www.
vecchiavarenna.it; Contrada Scoscesa 14;
meals €35-45; ☺12.30-2pm & 7.30-9.30pm
Tue-Sun)

Osteria Quatro Pass   ITALIAN €€

Places that don't have a lake view in
Varenna are at a distinct disadvan-
tage, which is why this place works
just that extra bit harder with the

Local Life
Il Gatto Nero

Situated high above Cernobbio,
Gatto Nero (Map p118, B6; ☑031 51
20 42; www.ristorantegattonero.com; Via
Monte Santo 69, Rovenna; meals €42-
75; ☺noon-2pm & 7.30-10pm Wed-Sun,
7.30-10pm Tue) is the jet set's restaurant of choice for good reason.
Book a front-row table beneath a
billowing canopy and you'll have
truly heavenly views of the lake
stretching out far below. Inside,
terracotta floors, warm wood
panelling and glowing low lighting
continue the romantic mood. The
elegant Mediterranean menu is
light and full of subtle flavours.

---

food and service. Cured meats, lake
fish and other local specialities are
perfectly prepared and presented.
(☑0341 81 50 91; www.quattropass.
com; Via XX Settembre 20; meals €25-40;
☺noon-2pm & 7-10pm, closed Mon-Wed
winter)

Drinking

Il Molo   BAR

The tiny terrace of Bar Il Molo is
Varenna's most sought-after *aperitivi*
spot. It's raised above the water with
cracking views north right up the lake.
(☑0341 83 00 70; www.barilmolo.it; Via Riva
Garibaldi 14; ☺11am-1am Apr-Oct)

The Best of
Milan & the Lakes

Bellagio (p116), Lago di Como
FRANCESCO IACOBELLI / GETTY IMAGES ©

Best Walks
Historic Milan

🏃 The Walk

Ruled by the Caesars, Napoleon and Mussolini, Milan's strategic position has made for a fascinating history. Mercantile Milan invented the idea of the city-state, and the Edict of Milan (AD 313) ended the persecution of the Christians. From Roman origins to Republican ambitions and industrial pretensions, this walk takes you through Milan's most tumultuous events.

Start Piazza del Duomo; Ⓜ Duomo

Finish Piazza Sempione; Ⓜ Moscova

Length 3.2km; 1½ hours

🍴 Take a Break

Liberty-style Bar Magenta (p84) on Corso Magenta is a good midpoint stop for a coffee or a snack. Alternatively, plan to finish with a picnic in Parco Sempione or *aperitivo* (see p97) at Bar Bianco (p67).

Castello Sforzesco

ALLAN BAXTER / GETTY IMAGES ©

❶ The Duomo

Milan's pearly white **Duomo** (p24), covered in a pantheon of marble saints, is the third-largest cathedral in the world. A gift from Giangaleazzo Visconti, who started works in 1386, its centuries-long creation maps much of the history of Milan.

❷ Biblioteca Ambrosiana

Blazing an intellectual trail out of the Dark Ages, Cardinal Federico Borromeo founded one of Italy's greatest libraries, the **Biblioteca Ambrosiana** (p32), in 1609. Among its collection are pages from da Vinci's compendium of drawings, the *Codex Atlanticus.*

❸ San Lorenzo Columns

Roman Mediolanum once had its forum in Piazza Carrobbio. Nearby, the 16 Corinthian columns that now stand as portico to the **Basilica di San Lorenzo** (p95) were originally part of a Roman temple or bath. Nearby on Via Edmondo de Amicis are the ruins of the **amphitheatre**.

4 Basilica di Sant'Ambrogio

Sant'Ambrogio (p83) was built on a paleo-Christian burial site and houses the bones of Milan's favourite bishop, St Ambrose. Its mongrel Lombard Romanesque style speaks volumes of history. The oldest part is the apse, featuring 4th-century mosaics depicting the *Miracle of St Ambrose*.

5 Tempio della Vittoria

Around the corner from the basilica, the **Temple of Victory** commemorates 10,000 victims of the 'Great War', WWI. Designed by Giovanni Munzio, its unadorned appearance caused much controversy in depressed, postwar Milan.

6 Civico Museo Archeologico

Foundation walls of Roman Milan and a medieval tower form part of Milan's **Archaeo-logical Museum** (p83), which houses a model of the Roman city and precious remnants of glass, grave goods and jewellery.

7 Castello Sforzesco

The **Castello Sforzesco** (p56), a turreted castle, embodies Milan's chameleon-like survival instincts. The art within it charts the rise and fall of the city's fortunes.

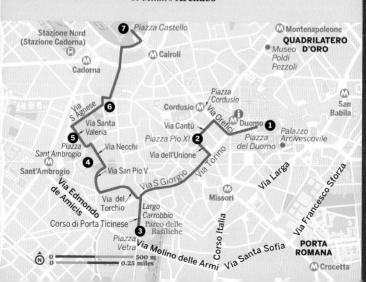

Best Walks
Designer Capital

🏃 The Walk

Milan's grab bag of architectural styles marks the city's restless evolution into a modern metropolis, from neoclassical shopping malls and baroque *palazzi* (mansions) to 19th-century boulevards lined with Liberty-style apartments and rationalist villas. Take a stroll through the architectural fashions on this walk.

Start Piazza del Duomo; Ⓜ Duomo

Finish Piazza Duca d'Aosta; Ⓜ Centrale FS

Length 4.5 km; two hours

🍴 Take a Break

Stop in the Quad for a stylish cappuccino and a mini *cornetto* (croissant) at the Fashion District's oldest cafe, Pasticceria Cova (p42). For lunch and evening *aperitivo*, press on to the HClub Diana (p48).

Casa degli Omenoni

❶ Galleria Vittorio Emanuele II

The glass-and-steel **gallery** (p31) is the direct progenitor of the modern shopping mall. It is home to some of the oldest shops and cafes in Milan, including **Camparino in Galleria**, founded in 1867, and **Savini**, where Charlie Chaplin declared 'I've never eaten so well'.

❷ Casa degli Omenoni

Wander north to Via degli Omenoni to enjoy the marvellous giants holding up the balcony of the **Casa degli Omenoni** (House of the Telamons), a 16th-century artist's residence. The vigorous Michelangelesque giants with their bulging muscles and bent backs became a reference for Milanese decorative architecture.

❸ Quadrilatero d'Oro

Lined with global marques, Via Monte Napoleone is the heart of the **Fashion District**. It follows the line of the old Roman wall and was once filled with small grocers and haberdasheries, which served the stately mansions. Look out for **Palazzo Melzi di Cusano**, **Palazzo Gavazzi** and **Museo Bagatti Valsecchi** (p43) with its fabulous Renaissance home decor.

 4 Villa Necchi Campiglio

After the Great War, Milan's architects embraced the brave new world of modernism. None more so than Piero Portaluppi, whose signature style of art deco and rationalist rigour is stamped all over town. A highlight is the **Villa Necchi Campiglio** (p46) which boasts a terrarium, radical electronic shutters and Milan's first domestic swimming pool.

5 Casa Galimberti

Tracing the eastern boundary of the Giardini Pubblici, Europe's first public park, Corso Venezia is lined with neoclassical and Liberty-style palaces. The area reached its fashionable zenith in the 1920s when art nouveau was all the rage. On Via Malpighi, **Casa Galimberti** (p50; No 3) typifies the style with its exuberant ceramic facade and twirling wrought-iron balconies.

6 Pirelloni

End at the Mesopotamian-style **Stazione Centrale** (p73). Adorned with winged horses, medallions and mosaic panelling, it is the largest train station in Italy. In answer to its fanciful art deco formula, Giò Ponti's sleek **Torre Pirelli** (1955–60) stands opposite, shooting skywards with a graceful, modern lightness.

Best
Fashion

Milan began to turn heads after WWII when Italy's fashion industry outgrew the workshops of Florence. Today the roll-call of designers in the Quadrilatero d'Oro makes for a glamorous jaunt for any fashion addict. Paris, New York and London may have equally influential designers but they can't compete with an industry town that lives and breathes fashion and takes retail as seriously as it does biotech or engineering.

RICHARD I'ANSON / GETTY IMAGES ©

Big-Brand Allergy

Younger labels and multibrand retailers can be found in Brera, Corso Como and Corso Vercelli. Giant department store Rinascente offers diffusion labels for men, women and children. For the Milanese version of high-street shopping, try Porta Ticinese, Via Torino and Corso Buenos Aires; but for Milan's most alternative and avant-garde shopping, head to Navigli and Zona Tortona.

Best Only in Milan

Antica Barbieria Colla Specialists in the finest quality men's grooming products. (p37)

Mutinelli The oldest milliner in Milan is filled with stylish headgear. (p51)

La Vetrina di Beryl 'Barbara's shoe store' to shoe cultists around the world. (p69)

Best Stylist's Eye

Wait and See Offbeat fashion brands from around the world. (p36)

Atelier Bergnach Made-to-measure skirts in a dazzling array of fabrics, shapes and styles. (p51)

Ziio Fashion jewellery with an Eastern flavour, as modelled by Queen Rania of Jordan. (p76)

Best Designer Discounts

DMagazine Last season's designer wear deeply discounted. (p53)

Cavalli e Nastri Carefully curated early mid-20th-century Italian fashion label. (p68)

Bivio Buy-sell-trade store selling top-quality 'pre-owned' fashion from big labels. (p101)

Best Concept Stores

10 Corso Como Milan's most hyped concept store is stuffed with weird and wonderful things. (p77)

Nonostantemarras The creative world of Antonio Marras. (p89)

Biffi Edgier trends and international heavy-weights. (p101)

Best
Design

Milan today is home to all the major design showrooms, the site of an endless round of influential international design fairs, and continues to be a centre of design education and publishing. Design here isn't merely functional (although the modernist ideal of creating useful objects is always at its core); it is suffused with emotion – expressive, inventive, humorous and individual.

PAOLO CORDELLI / GETTY IMAGES ©

Who's Who

A visit to the Design Museum at the Triennale di Milano is a wonderful way to pay homage to the work of Italy's best and brightest. Many of these called, or continue to call, Milan home. Names to watch for include Giò Ponti, Bruno Munari, Piero Fornasetti, Enzo Mari, the Castiglioni brothers, Gaetano Pesce, Mario Bellini, Gae Aulenti, Ettore Sottsass and Alessandro Mendini.

Best Design Inspiration

Triennale di Milano Museum, educational facility and showroom, the Triennale has championed design since the 1930s. (p63)

Studio Museo Achille Castiglioni Tour the studio of one of Italy's most influential 20th-century designers. (p63)

Design Library Flick through pages of classic designs in back issues of *Domus*, *Abitare* and *Ottogono*. (p89)

Superstudio Più Epicentre of the furniture fair's fringe shows, with a dazzling schedule of exhibits and parties. (www.superstudiogroup.com; Via Tortona 27; Ⓜ Porta Genova)

Best Design Shops

Spazio Rossana Orlandi An iconic interior-design 'space' with out-of-the-ordinary objects and homewares. (p87)

Alessi All your favourite Alessi homewares are housed in this flagship store designed by Martí Guixé. (p43)

MUST Shop Form and function meet happily in Museo Nazionale della Scienza e della Tecnologia's imaginative on-site shop. (p87)

Moroni Gomma *The* place to go for highly styled, one-off keepsakes and design-inspired souvenirs. (p36)

Best **Eating**

Milan's dining scene is much like its fashion scene, with new restaurant openings hotly debated and seats at Michelin-starred tables hard to come by. Whether it's dyed-in-the-wool traditional or contemporary fusion cuisine you're after, you'll eat some of Italy's most memorable and sophisticated food here.

REDA & CO SRL / ALAMY ©

Best Modern Italian

La Brisa Contemporary gastronomy at its unfussy best, set in a beautiful courtyard garden. (p84)

Un Posto a Milano Deceptively simple home cooking dished up in a farmhouse garden. (p103)

Alice Ristorante Award-winning chef Viviana Varese's exciting new restaurant atop Eataly's new flagship store. (p73)

La Veranda The discreet signature restaurant of the Four Seasons Hotel. (p43)

Best Classics

Bagutta Going strong since 1920; now considered a Historical Landmark. (p45)

Osteria del Treno This working railway club with a Liberty ballroom continues to serve authentic dishes at fair prices. (p73)

Trattoria Milanese A true trattoria serving a repertoire of classics in one of the oldest parts of town. (p33)

La Bettola di Piero A neighbourhood restaurant with a Slow Food philosophy and uncompromisingly good food. (p103)

Latteria di San Marco A classic family concern with Arturo in the kitchen and his wife and daughters waiting table. (p65)

Best Gelati

Gelato Giusto Inventive flavours dreamed up by a Maître Chocolatier. (p46)

☑ **Top Tips**

▶ All high-end and popular restaurants should be booked ahead, especially for Friday and Saturday evenings and Sunday lunch.

▶ Book ahead for *all* meals during Salone del Mobile (Furniture Fair) and Fashion Week.

Artico Gelateria Watch the magic happen behind the counter at this neighbourhood gelateria. (p74)

Shockolat Playing flavour favourite with milk, dark, white, chilli, *gianduja* (chocolate-hazelnut) and cinnamon chocolate. (p85)

Best
Shopping

Milan's shopping scene is diverse and vibrant, spanning the spectrum from artisanal ateliers to concept shops and lifestyle stores. Guilds ranging across jewellers, bakers, carpenters and milliners have catered to the European aristocracy for centuries, so quality and choice are appropriately superb.

RENAULT PHILIPPE / GETTY IMAGES ©

Best Food & Wine

Peck Historic Peck is crammed with speciality meats, cheeses, oils, pastas, chocolates and wine. (p37)

N'Ombra de Vin More than 3000 labels in the cellars of an Augustinian refectory. (p66)

Eataly This Slow Food emporium housed in a former theatre is full of rare treats. (p77)

Best Independent Designers

Monica Castiglioni Self-taught jeweller and daughter of design great Achille Castiglioni. (p77)

Risi Style without excess; Risi is everything the Milanese love. (p86)

Mauro Leone Originally from Turin, Mauro has won Milanese hearts with

his fashionable and affordable footwear. (p101)

Malìparmi Prints, beading and embroidery in sunshine colours make Malìparmi a summer must-have. (p69)

Best Heritage Brands

Borsalino Maker of the world's coolest hats for more than 150 years. (p36)

Pellini Unique costume jewellery and hairpieces from the granddaughters of a Teatro alla Scala costumier. (p50)

Aspesi Understated, stylish outdoor gear for weekends hiking and boating on the lakes. (p43)

Doriani Cashmere knitwear and light-weft polo shirts keep Doriani's gentlemen clients looking effortlessly cool. (p53)

☑ **Top Tips**

▶ Opening hours are from 3pm to 7pm Monday and 10am to 7pm from Tuesday to Saturday; some smaller shops take a lunch break from 12.30pm to 3pm.

▶ Non-EU citizens can claim back the Value Added Tax (VAT) on purchases more than €154.94 at stores displaying a 'Tax Free Shopping' sign. Claim your refund at Rinascente department store's tax-free centre or at the airport.

Best
Drinking

Like everything in Milan, drinking is a stylish affair and an opportunity to make *la bella figura* (a good impression). *Aperitivo* (happy hour) stretches from 6pm to 9pm, though the Milanese rarely get there before 7pm. Expect your cocktails to be expertly mixed and accompanied by a tasty, complimentary and sometimes fabulous buffet. Finally, getting drunk or otherwise messy is *molto vulgare* (very vulgar).

MIMMO LOBEFARO / ALAMY ©

Best Big-Night-Out Aperitivo

Bulgari Hotel Expect vintage liquors, expertly mixed cocktails and highbrow *aperitivo*. (p68)

Ceresio 7 Milan's coolest *aperitivo* spot is beside the pool atop the old Enel (electricity company) HQ. (p74)

Grand Hotel des Iles Borromées Drink a manhattan on the terrace overlooking Lago Maggiore, just as Hemingway did. (p111)

Best Wine Cellars

N'Ombra de Vin Tastings can be had all day at the vaulted cellars. (p66)

Cantine Isola A neighbourhood bar with an exceptional list of limited-production regional wines. (p75)

SignorVino A wine merchant and restaurant that prepares meals to match its 600-bottle inventory. (p35)

La Bottiglieria del Castello Sip the finest regional wines in Intra's pretty cobbled piazza. (p111)

Best Cocktails

Camparino in Galleria A Milanese institution serving Campari-based cocktails since 1867. (p34)

Mag Café Creatively crafted cocktails in a laid-back bar with a speakeasy vibe. (p97)

Nottingham Forest Dario Comino is the alchemist behind this bar's seriously inventive cocktails. (p48)

Bar Rita An American-style cocktail bar serving up classics with a twist. (p97)

☑ **Top Tips**

▶ During happy hour drinks prices range from €8 to €10, but be prepared to fork out up to €15 or €20 at more luxe establishments. Usually the higher the drink price, the more lavish the buffet. At €8-plus you can expect to see platters of charcuterie and cheeses, *pizzetta*, salads and even pasta.

Best **Architecture**

JOSE FUSTE RAGA / CORBIS ©

Milan's architectural charm lies in its mix of styles, but at the fore is Italy's love affair with 20th-century art nouveau architecture. Wide streets are lined with elegant fin de siècle Liberty apartments that merge with 1930s rationalist rigour. Meanwhile, out of the postwar devastation two of the world's most avant-garde skyscrapers arose in the form of BBPR's Torre Velasca and Giò Ponti's Torre Pirelli.

Best Exteriors

Duomo Cloud-piercing Gothic spires in cloudy Candoglian marble. (p24)

Villa Olmo Neoclassical Olmo, with its impressive colonnaded facade, was remodelled in the 'modern fashion'. (p120)

Stazione Centrale Deco-tinged, neo-Babylonian architecture epitomising the nationalist fervour of Fascism. (p73)

Torre Pirelli The tapered sides of Ponti's modernist icon shoot skywards with dynamic modernity. (Piazza Duca d'Aosta 3; Ⓜ Centrale FS)

Best Interior Decor

Villa Necchi Campiglio Restored 1930s villa designed by rationalist architect Piero Portaluppi. (p46)

Chiesa di Santa Maria Presso di San Satiro Bramante's trompe l'œil apse plays cleverly with perspective. (p32)

Portinari Chapel Milan's finest Renaissance chapel has masterly frescoes by Vincenzo Foppa. (p95)

Casa Museo Boschi-di Stefano An art deco apartment with postwar furnishings and artworks by De Chirico. (p45)

Palazzo Borromeo Every inch of the luxurious interiors of this over-the-top Borromean palace are painted, stuccoed, gilded and inlaid with precious marbles. (p107)

Best Museums

Fondazione Prada An artfully renovated industrial complex by visionary Dutch architect Rem Koolhaas. (p103)

Il Grande Museo del Duomo Guido Canali's new interiors showcase the Duomo's architectural accessories stunningly. (p31)

Gallerie d'Italia The 18th- and 19th-century art collection of the San Paolo bank now hangs in three of Milan's most sumptuously decorated *palazzi*. (p32)

Best
History

The Romans didn't consider wild Cisalpine Gaul part of Italy at all. In 222 BC when they conquered the city of the Insubri Celts they named it Mediolanum (Middle of the Plains). Since then Milan has been home to imperial courts, supplied arms for various empires and flourished on the back of clever politicking, manufacturing and well-managed farming.

Best Roman Remains

Civico Museo Archeologico Home to Roman, Greek and Etruscan artefacts and a model of Roman Milan. (p83)

San Lorenzo Columns Sixteen free-standing columns salvaged from a Roman residence and now an *aperitivo* hot spot. (p95)

Best of Medieval Milan

Castello Sforzesco Milan's mighty medieval fortress is now the repository of splendid period artworks. (p56)

Biblioteca Ambrosiana Home to Leonardo da Vinci's priceless sketchbook, the *Codex Atlanticus*. (p32)

Basilica di Sant'Ambrogio Milan's spiritual home is filled with medieval masterpieces, a magnificent gold altar and a sky of gold. (p83)

Best of Renaissance Milan

The Last Supper Leonardo da Vinci's peerless mural depicting Christ at the moment he reveals his betrayal. (p80)

Chiesa di Santa Maria Presso di San Satiro Bramante's clever trick of false perspective turns a tiny chapel into a full-sized church. (p32)

Chiesa di San Maurizio Filled with fabulous frescoes from da Vinci's contemporary Bernardino Luini. (p83)

Best of 19th-Century Milan

Duomo Napoleon chose Milan as capital of his Cisalpine Empire and completed the Duomo, where he was crowned in 1805. (p24)

Palazzo Reale This Visconti palace is now a world-class museum, preserving one ruined hall as a grim reminder of WWII. (p31)

Cimitero Monumentale The final resting place of Milan's good burghers, including an epic memorial to those who died in WWII. (p73)

Best
Art

Milan's museums contain collections from the early Renaissance to neoclassical. What's more, you can often linger with a Bellini or Caravaggio without the usual crowds, even in Milan's most famous gallery, the Pinacoteca di Brera. The city is also a treasure trove of 20th-century art. At the Museo del Novecento, the work of futurists Umberto Boccioni and Giacomo Balla is, a hundred years on, still shockingly fresh.

NEIL SETCHFIELD / GETTY IMAGES ©

Best Frescoes

The Last Supper Not strictly a fresco at all; Leonardo da Vinci's *Last Supper* breaks all the rules. (p80)

Chiesa di San Maurizio Seventy years in the making, San Maurizio's frescoes still dazzle onlookers. (p83)

Portinari Chapel Vincenzo Foppa was a pioneer of the Renaissance in Lombardy, and these are his finest works. (p95)

Best Period Collections

Castello Sforzesco The Ancient Art Museum's collection includes Michelangelo's moving *Rondanini Pietà*. (p56)

Pinacoteca di Brera A staggering roll-call of masters from Titian and Tintoretto to Caravaggio. (p58)

Museo Poldi Pezzoli Renaissance treasures displayed in artful, historically styled rooms. (p40)

Museo Bagatti Valsecchi The Bagatti Valsecchi *palazzo* is a living museum of the Quattrocento. (p43)

Gallerie d'Italia A vast collection paying homage to 18th- and 19th-century Lombard painting. (p32)

Best 20th-Century Greats

Museo del Novecento Has 4000 sq metres designed by Italo Rota to showcase Italy's 20th-century talent. (p28)

Villa Necchi Campiglio Home of Pavian heiresses, Nedda and Gigina, who had a canny eye for big-ticket artworks. (p46)

Casa Museo Boschi-di Stefano Find 20th-century greats crowded salon-style in a Piero Portaluppi–designed apartment. (p45)

Best Private Foundations

Fondazione Nicola Trussardi Trussardi's foundation creates contemporary shows in unusual public venues. (p51)

Fondazione Prada Prada's contemporary-art collection is now housed in a visually stunning space designed by Rem Koolhaas. (p103)

Best
Culture

The city of Verdi and Puccini has been home to some of the world's foremost classical musicians for at least two centuries. Also home to Italy's major music publishers, Milan is on the international tour circuit of the best European and North American music acts, theatre companies and dance troupes. In summer the city hosts an impressive series of cultural events.

RICHARD I'ANSON / GETTY IMAGES ©

Best Music

Teatro alla Scala Dress up for a night of ballet or opera at Italy's most famous theatre. (p35)

Auditorium di Milano Home of the legendary Giuseppe Verdi Orchestra. (p98)

Blue Note The largest and most prestigious of Milan's jazz venues. (p76)

Nibada Theatre A tiny venue with a big heart and stellar blues, soul and folk acts. (p99)

Best Festivals

Carnevale Ambrosiano Lent comes late to Milan with Carnival held on Saturday (after everyone else's Fat Tuesday) in Piazza del Duomo.

Festa del Naviglio Music, food, parades and special events are held along the canals in Navigli's June festival.

Festa di Sant'Ambrogio The feast day of Milan's patron saint is celebrated on 7 December with a huge Christmas fair.

Best Exhibitions

Palazzo Reale Hosts world-class art exhibitions from the likes of da Vinci, Chagall, Dario Fo and Warhol. (p31)

Palazzo della Ragione New contemporary-photography venue showcasing established and up-coming talent. (p32)

Fondazione Prada Miuccia Prada's namesake gallery hosts exciting contemporary-art shows and installations. (p103)

Triennale di Milano Championing design in all its forms with rotating permanent and temporary exhibits. (p63)

Best Theatre

Piccolo Teatro Grassi A risk-taking repertory with a program of ballet and Commedia dell'Arte. (p36)

Piccolo Teatro Strehler Generally acknowledged as the city's top theatre venue. (p68)

Best
Nightlife

Milan's nightlife traverses the spectrum from blandly commercial to cutting edge, but glamming up applies across the board. Entry runs from €10 to upwards of €20. While club popularity is surprisingly stable (Plastic has been in the business for 24 years), keeping up with nights and DJs is not easy. *Zero's* fortnightly guide and online info is useful (http://zero.eu/milano), as is Milano2night (www.milanotonight.it).

GIOVANNI TAGINI / ALAMY ©

Best Big Nights Out

Plastic According to Andy Warhol, the sexiest and most transgressive club in town. Located south of the centre off Via Ripamonte. (Via Gargano 15; ⏰11pm-5am Fri-Sat, to 3am Sun; ❄; 🚋24)

Alcatraz Founded by Italian rockstar Vasco Rossi, this 1800-sq-metre garage rocks a huge weekend crowd. (p74)

Tunnel Top DJs spin beneath the railway tracks of the Stazione Centrale. (p76)

Best Live Music

Blue Note Part of a venerable international jazz franchise, with some soul, blues and world music thrown in. (p76)

Nibada Theatre The place to go for serious blues, soul, folk and rock-and-roll bands. (p99)

Scimmie Emerging jazz and alternative-rock bands play at this canalside venue. (p98)

La Salumeria della Musica This music 'deli' hosts up-and-coming artists alongside big names such as Noel

☑ Top Tips

▶ Go late and dress to impress; you won't get past the door police if you fail to make *la bella figura* (a good impression).

▶ Most clubs mix straight and gay. Even at landmark gay-and-lesbian bars most nights are straight friendly.

Gallagher. South of the centre off Via Ripamonti. (www.lasalumeriadella musica.com; Via Pasinetti 4; ⏰9pm-2am Mon-Sat Sep-Jun; ❄; 🚋24)

Best
Lake Experiences

Sprinkled with pretty villages, palm trees and dark cypress groves, the Italian lakes have been a favoured holiday destination since the Romans planted olive trees and built the first holiday villas around their shores. Since then writers, princes, aristrocrats and celebrities have beaten a path here, filling the grand Liberty hotels and wandering lakeside promenades.

JOSE FUSTE RAGA / CORBIS ©

Best Outdoor Activities

Aero Club Como Flying planes over the lake since 1913. Now you can buzz Bellagio in your very own Cessna. (p122)

Lido di Villa Olmo Grab a lounger on the 'beach' or cool off in the world's most scenic public pool. (p121)

Barindelli's Make a tour of Lago di Como James Bond–style in a mahogany cigarette boat. (p117)

Bicicò Mountain-bike down Monte Mottarone to Stresa, enjoying bird's-eye views over Lago Maggiore (p110)

Funicolare Como–Brunate Swing high above Lago di Como in a glass-sided gondola. (p122)

Best Lakeside Dining

Casabella Perfectly grilled lake fish with views over the water to match. (p107)

Locanda di Orta Michelin-starred magic converts Lago d'Orta ingredients into works of food art. (p113)

Il Gatto Nero Enjoy some movie-star magic in George Clooney's favourite Lago di Como restaurant. (p125)

Vecchia Varenna Savour gnocchi and truffles while dabbling your toes in the water on this lakeside terrace. (p125)

Best Museums

Palazzo Borromeo Set against 10 tiered terraces of blooming flowers, the palace houses Old Masters such as Rubens, Titian and Mantegna. (p107)

Villa Olmo Blockbuster art shows adorn the Liberty-style interiors of Lake Como's grandest neoclassical villa. (p120)

Villa Carlotta Strung with paintings and home to Canova's alabaster sculpture *Cupid and Psyche*. (p124)

Survival Guide

Survival Guide

Before You Go

When to Go

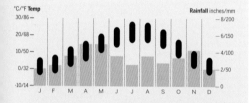

°C/°F Temp
Rainfall inches/mm

30/86 — — 8/200

20/68 — — 6/150

10/50 — — 4/100

0/32 — — 2/50

-10/14 — — 0

J F M A M J J A S O N D

➡ **Winter (Nov–Mar)**
The feast of St Ambrose heralds the start of opera season. Epiphany follows, with the procession of the Three Kings, and February is Carnivale.

➡ **Spring (Apr–Jun)**
Salone del Mobile (Furniture Fair) turns Milan into a madhouse in April. Escape to the lakes.

➡ **Summer (Jul & Aug)**
Summer is hot, so Milanese escape the city to lakeside villas or mountain chalets.

➡ **Autumn (Sep & Oct)**
Balmy autumn days kick off new exhibitions and fashion shows.

Book Your Stay

☑ **Top Tip** If you're visiting during the Salone del Mobile or any of the fashion shows, you'll need to book at least a month in advance, if not more.

➡ Milan is an industry town catering to business professionals, which means there's plenty of high-end designer accommodation and very few bargains.

➡ Some prime hotels are located for easy access to the Fiera, but aren't always convenient for tourists. Check before you book.

➡ Cheaper accommodation can be found in Navigli, but watch out for clubs nearby and book your room accordingly.

➡ For character, value and a quiet residential vibe, seek out hotels in Brera, San Babila and around the Giardini Pubblici.

Useful Websites

Lonely Planet (www.lonelyplanet.com) Author-recommendation reviews and online booking.

Airbnb (www.airbnb.com) Rent apartments and studios direct from owners for the best savings in town.

Hotels in Milan (www.hotelsinmilan.it) The leading provider of hotel and B&B bookings in Milan.

Visita Milano (www.visitamilano.it) Provincial tourist website with information on accommodation, transport and attractions.

Best Budget

Vietnamonamour (www.vietnamonamour.com) Vibrant rooms with a splash of Vietnamese colour.

Ostello Bello (www.ostellobello.com) A community hub with cool communal spaces, and shared and private rooms.

Foresteria Cascina Cuccagna (www.cuccagna.org) A country-style guesthouse with dorms and doubles.

Casa Mia (www.hotelcasa-mia.com) Contemporary rooms close to the Giardini Pubblici.

Best Midrange

Casa Titta (www.casatitta.it) Home from home in a 1920s apartment.

LaFavia Four Rooms (http://lafavia4rooms.com) Designer-styled rooms looking out on a leafy roof terrace.

Foresteria Monforte (www.foresteriamonforte.it) Three classy rooms with a minimalist, modern vibe.

Hotel Gran Duca di York (www.ducadiyork.com) Art nouveau elegance within a stone's throw of the Duomo.

Antica Locanda Leonardo (www.anticalocandaleonardo.com) Period furniture and parquet floors in a 19th-century residence.

Best Top End

Armani Hotel Milano (http://milan.armanihotels.com) A temple to Armani's understated luxurious style.

Palazzo Segreti (www.palazzosegreti.com) A 19th-century palace with shockingly modern interiors.

Maison Borella (www.hotelmaisonborella.com) The only hotel in Milan overlooking the Naviglio Grande canal.

Hotel Spadari Duomo (www.spadarihotel.com) Rooms at the Spadari are minigalleries showcasing emerging artists.

3Rooms (www.10corsocomo.com) Design-styled mansion suites in the 10 Corso Como complex.

Arriving in Milan

☑ **Top Tip** For the best way to get to your accommodation, see p17.

Malpensa Airport

➡ **Malpensa International Airport** (MXP; ☏ 02 23 23 23; www.milanomalpensa-airport.com) is 50km northwest of the city centre.

➡ **Malpensa Express** (☏ 02 7249 4949; www.malpensaexpress.it; one way €12)

Departs every 30 minutes from Terminal 1 to Stazione Centrale (€10, 52 minutes) and Cadorna's Stazione Nord (€11, 40 minutes) between 6.50am and 9.20pm. Passengers arriving into Terminal 2 will need to catch a shuttle bus to the Terminal 1 train station.

➡ **Malpensa Shuttle** (www.malpensashuttle.it; one way/return €10/16) Runs between the airport and Piazza Luigi di Savoia outside Stazione Centrale, every 20 minutes from 5am to 10.30am, and approximately hourly throughout the rest of the night (tickets €10, 45 minutes).

➡ **Taxi** There is a flat fee of €90 between Malpensa and Milan. The drive from Milan should take 50 minutes outside peak hours. For travellers to Terminal 2, this might prove the quickest option.

Linate Airport

Located 7km east of the city, **Linate Airport** (LIN; ☏02 23 23 23; www.milanolinate-airport.com) handles European and domestic flights.

➡ **Starfly** (☏02 5858 7237; www.airportbusexpress.it; one way/return €5/9) Runs

between the airport and Stazione Centrale every 30 minutes between 5.30am and 10pm. Tickets are sold on the bus (€5, 25 minutes).

➡ **Bus 73** (www.atm-mi.it) This city bus departs from Piazza San Babila every 10 to 15 minutes (€1.50, 25 minutes) between 6am and 9.30pm. Tickets can be purchased on board.

Stazione Centrale

International high-speed trains from France and Switzerland arrive in Milan's **Stazione Centrale** (Central Station; Piazza Duca d'Aosta).

➡ To reach Piazza del Duomo from here take metro line M3 to Duomo.

➡ To reach Castello Sforzesco take metro line M2 to Cadorna.

➡ To reach Navigli take metro line M2 to Porta Genova.

Getting Around

Milan has an efficient integrated public-transport system (ATM; www.atm-mi.it)

of metro, trams and buses, but when you're moving around the historic centre you'll probably find it more convenient to walk. Trams are a good way to see the city while covering more ground.

Bicycle

☑ **Best for...** Touring the historic centre and scooting about Parco Sempione.

➡ **BikeMi** (www.bikemi.it) Milan's public bike network. Anyone can pick up and drop off bikes at bike stands throughout the city. Daily, weekly or annual passes are available online, by phone (☏02 4860 7607) or at the ATM Infopoints.

Boat

☑ **Best for...** Cruising the canals and getting around the lakes without the hassle of driving and with better views.

➡ **Navigli Lombardi** (www.naviglilombardi.it) Runs sightseeing cruises along Milan's canals between April and September.

➡ **Navigazione Laghi** (www.navigazionelaghi.it) Operates ferries and hydrofoils on the Italian lakes. You can check timetables, prices and book tickets online.

Car & Motorcycle

☑ **Best for...** Out-of-season lake touring.

→ It simply isn't worth having a car in Milan. The city is small, easily walkable and parking is a nightmare. If you do have a car, it's best to leave it in a guarded car park, most of which charge €15 to €40 for 24 hours.

→ Street parking costs €2 per hour in the centre. To pay, buy a SostaMilano card from a tobacconist; scratch off the date and time, and display it in your window.

→ Beware: many streets are pedestrianised or have restricted access.

→ Having a car to tour the lakes is great out of season, but inadvisable during the summer and holiday weekends, when traffic can slow to a crawl.

→ Enquire after parking when you book your accommodation, as not all hotels have garage facilities.

Tickets & Passes

Milan's public-transport system is inexpensive and efficient. Metro, trams and buses all use the same kind of ticket. You can only buy these tickets from metro stations, tobacconists or newsagents, or through the ATM app, never from the driver. On buses and trams it's the traveller's responsibility to validate their ticket. If you're caught riding without a ticket that's been clearly stamped you will be fined €37. For ease of use and to avoid the hassle of validating tickets, simply opt for single or multiday passes:

→ **Basic ticket** Valid for 90 minutes; €1.50

→ **One-day ticket** Valid for 24 hours; €4.50

→ **Carnet of 10 tickets** Valid for 90 minutes each; €13.80

→ **Evening ticket** Valid from 8pm until the end of service; €3

Metro

☑ **Best for...** Quick transport between major sights, connecting to the train station and venturing outside the main tourist areas.

→ The metro operates between 6am and 12.30am.

→ There are four underground lines; the red line (M1) connects the Duomo with Porta Venezia, Castello Sforzesco and Corso Magenta; the green line (M2) connects Porta Garibaldi and Brera to Navigli; the yellow line (M3) connects the Quad with Porta Romana;

and the lilac line (M5) connects Porta Garibaldi with Isola.

→ A ticket costs €1.50 and is valid for one metro ride or up to 90 minutes on ATM buses and trams.

→ Tickets are sold at electronic ticket machines within the stations, or at tobacconists and newsstands.

→ There are various good-value travel passes available.

→ Download the free ATM app for network maps, timetables and tickets, which can be purchased using either a credit card or PayPal.

Tram & Bus

☑ **Best for...** Scenic rides, connecting to attractions off the metro lines, and for travellers who can't easily walk long distances.

➡ ATM oversees trams and an extensive bus network.

➡ Route maps are available from ATM Infopoints and at news-stands in the metro stops.

➡ Tickets are sold at metro stations, tobacconists and news-stands and are valid on buses, trams and metro trains.

➡ Tickets must be pre-purchased and validated when boarding.

➡ Tram 1 is a retro orange beauty with wooden seats and original fittings. It runs along Via Settembrini before cutting through the historic centre along Via Manzoni and back towards Castello Sforzesco.

➡ Trams 2 and 3 are good for sightseeing. Tram 9 loops round the town from Porta Genova to Porta Venezia.

➡ Tram ATMosfera has been renovated to

incorporate a restaurant where you can eat your way through a five-course menu as you tour the city. It departs from Piazza Castello at 1pm and 8pm from Tuesday to Sunday. Tickets cost €70. Book online (http://atmosfera.atm.it/reservation).

➡ Night services run between 12.30am and 2.30am. There is no service between 2.30am and 6am.

Taxi

☑ **Best for...** Arriving at high-end dinner options and the theatre, and for late-night rides back to your hotel.

➡ Taxis cost around €10 for the average short trip.

➡ Taxis must be picked up at designated ranks, usually outside train stations, large hotels and major piazzas; they cannot be hailed.

➡ You can call for a cab on ☎02 40 40, ☎02 69 69 or ☎02 85 85. English is spoken.

➡ Be aware that when you call for a cab the meter runs from receipt of call, not pick up.

➡ There's a fixed rate price for the airports.

Train

☑ **Best for...** Travel to suburban parts of the city and travel to the lakes.

➡ Stresa and Como on the southern shores of Lago Maggiore and Lago di Como respectively are served by fast trains from Milan.

➡ Stresa is on the Domodossola–Milan train line (€8.30 to €9, 75 minutes).

➡ Como San Giovanni station is served by trains from Stazione Centrale (€4.80 to €13, 30 to 60 minutes).

➡ Como's lakeside Stazione FNM (listed on timetables as Como Nord Lago) is served by trains from Cadorna (€4.10, one hour).

Essential Information

Business Hours

Many shops and restaurants close on Monday or are only open from 3pm to 7pm. All civic museums are also closed on Monday. Many smaller shops and restaurants also close for several weeks in August.

Discounts

➡ To save cash, purchase a three-day cumulative ticket (€12) for Milan's nine admission-charging civic museums (www. turismo.milano.it). Tickets can be purchased online or at any of the museums.

➡ For longer stays, consider a Milano Card worth €35. Valid for a year, it gives access to all the civic museums as often as you like, as well as granting discounts on entry at Palazzo Reale, Palazzo della Ragione and Padiglione d'Arte Contemporania (PAC) exhibitions.

➡ The most comprehensive discount card is the MilanoCard (24-hours/ three days €6.50/13; www.milanocard.it), which offers free public transport, priority access to *The Last Supper*, skip-the-queue priority at the Duomo, as well as free access to the civic museums and between 20% and 50% discount on a range of other participating museums, selected restaurants and airport

buses. Buy the card online and then pick it up from Stazione Centrale or the airport.

Electricity

Plugs are standard European two round pins:

➡ Voltage 220V

➡ Frequency 50Hz

➡ Cycle AC

220V/50Hz

Emergency

24-hour pharmacy (☎02 669 07 35; Stazione Centrale, upper gallery)

Ambulance (☎118)

Carabinieri (☎112)

EU-wide emergency hotline (☎112)

Fire (☎115)

Municipal Police (☎027 72 71)

Money

☑ **Top Tip** ATMs are widely available. However, if you need to change some cash, post offices and banks offer the best rates. Exchange offices keep longer hours, but watch for higher commissions. To change money you'll need to present your passport as ID.

Currency

➡ The euro (€) is Italy's currency. Notes come in denominations of €500, €200, €100, €50, €20, €10 and €5.

Credit Cards

➡ Visa and MasterCard are among the most widely recognised, but others such as Cirrus and Maestro are also accepted. American Express and Diners Club are not universally accepted, so check in advance.

Tipping

➡ If service isn't included on the bill, leave a 10% to 15% tip. In bars, most Italians just leave small change (€0.10 to €0.20 is fine). Tipping taxi drivers isn't normal practice, but you should tip porters and staff at high-end hotels.

Money-Saving Tips

To make the most of your euros consider the following:

➡ Forget taxis – take the Malpensa Express from the airport to the city, then use the metro.

➡ Buy unlimited day passes for public transport or the MilanoCard.

➡ When it comes to eating, don't feel you have to order multiple courses.

➡ Local trattorias offer the best-value meals. Anything with a designer look will come with a designer price tag.

➡ Get into the swing of *aperitivo*, where for the price of a cocktail (€8) you can graze the buffet bar.

➡ If you book ahead, you can secure the cheaper seats at Teatro alla Scala (€25 to €40).

Public Holidays

☑ **Top Tip** If you're in town over Easter, remember to stock up the fridge or reserve a table for a slap-up lunch on Easter Sunday.

Banks, offices and some shops will be closed on public holidays. Restaurants, museums and tourist attractions tend to stay open.

New Year's Day
1 January

Epiphany 6 January

Easter Monday
March/April

Liberation Day 25 April

Labour Day 1 May

Republic Day 2 June

Feast of the Assumption 15 August

All Saints Day
1 November

Festa di Sant'Ambrogio
7 December

Feast of the Immaculate Conception
8 December

Christmas Day
25 December

Festa di San Stefano
26 December

Safe Travel

Milan is a safe and affluent destination; however, as with any major city, pickpocketing can be an issue at busy train stations and Piazza del Duomo. If you're the victim of theft or crime, simply find the nearest police station and report the incident. For insurance purposes you'll need to fill in any relevant forms. For lost or stolen passports, contact your embassy.

Telephone

☑ **Top Tip** Widespread city wi-fi means using free internet call services such as Skype and Viber is easy.

Italy uses GSM 900/1800, which is compatible with the rest of Europe and Australia but not with North American GSM 1900 or the Japanese system.

Mobile Phones

➡ To buy a SIM card you'll need to supply your passport and the address of your accommodation.

➡ The main mobile-phone providers are Telecom Italia Mobile (TIM), Wind and Vodafone.

Country & City Codes

➡ The dialling code for Italy is ☎39. The city code for Milan is ☎02, which precedes local numbers. The city code is an integral part of the number and must always be dialled.

➡ Mobile-phone numbers begin with a three-digit prefix such as ☎330.

➡ Toll-free (free-phone) numbers are known as *numeri verdi* and usually start with ☎800.

Tourist Information

Milan Tourist Office

(☎02 8845 6555; www. turismo.milano.it; Galleria Vittorio Emanuele II 11-12; ⏰9am-7pm Mon-Fri, to 6pm Sat, 10am-6pm Sun; Ⓜ Duomo) Has a good supply of maps, brochures and tours. The office maintains listings of hotels, but there's no booking facility.

Travellers with Disabilities

Milan is not an easy destination for disabled travellers. But for those with limited mobility, ATM has recently introduced low-floor buses on many of its routes, and some metro stations are equipped with lifts. See the dual-language **Milano Per Tutti** (www.milanopertutti.it) for details and for itineraries of accessible sights.

Dos & Don'ts

➡ Do dress fashionably. Appearance is important.

➡ Do greet people with *buongiorno* (good day) or *buona sera* (good evening).

➡ Do tip hotel porters and helpful staff in high-end hotels.

➡ Do take a beautifully wrapped gift of chocolates or pastries if invited to a Milanese home.

➡ Don't disrespect meal times; restaurants won't stretch to accommodate late arrivals.

➡ Don't mess with the merchandise. If you want to see something in a shop, ask for assistance.

➡ Don't think you have to order three courses (antipasto, *primo* and *secondo*) at every meal. Italians don't.

➡ Don't assume you can purchase tickets on board buses and trams; they must be bought beforehand.

Visas

Generally not required for stays of up to 90 days (or at all for EU nationals); some nationalities need a Schengen visa. To check the visa requirements for your country, see www.schengenvisainfo.com/tourist-schengen-visa.

Language

Standard Italian is taught and spoken throughout Italy. Regional dialects are an important part of identity in many parts of the country, but you'll have no trouble being understood anywhere if you stick to standard Italian, which we've also used in this chapter.

The sounds used in spoken Italian can all be found in English. If you read our pronunciation guides as if they were English, you'll be understood. The stressed syllables are indicated with italics. Note that *ai* is pronounced as in 'aisle', *ay* as in 'say', *ow* as in 'how', *dz* as the 'ds' in 'lids', and that *r* is a strong and rolled sound.

To enhance your trip with a phrase-book, visit **lonelyplanet.com**. Lonely Planet iPhone phrasebooks are available through the Apple App store.

Basics

Hello.
Buongiorno.　　bwon·*jor*·no

Goodbye.
Arrivederci.　　a·ree·ve·*der*·chee

How are you?
Come sta?　　*ko*·me sta

Fine. And you?
Bene. E Lei?　　*be*·ne e lay

Please.
Per favore.　　per fa·*vo*·re

Thank you.
Grazie.　　*gra*·tsye

Excuse me.
Mi scusi.　　mee *skoo*·zee

Sorry.
Mi dispiace.　　mee dees·*pya*·che

Yes./No.
Sì./No.　　see/no

I don't understand.
Non capisco.　　non ka·*pee*·sko

Do you speak English?
Parla inglese?　　*par*·la een·*gle*·ze

Eating & Drinking

I'd like ...　　*Vorrei ...*　　vo·*ray* ..

a coffee　　*un caffè*　　oon ka·*fe*

a table　　*un tavolo*　　oon ta·*vo*·lo

the menu　　*il menù*　　eel me·*noo*

two beers　　*due birre*　　*doo*·e *bee*·re

What would you recommend?
Cosa mi consiglia?　　*ko*·za mee kon·*see*·lya

Enjoy the meal!
Buon appetito!　　bwon a·pe·*tee*·to

That was delicious!
Era squisito!　　*e*·ra skwee·*zee*·to

Cheers!
Salute!　　sa·*loo*·te

Please bring the bill.
Mi porta il conto, per favore?　　mee *por*·ta eel *kon*·to per fa·*vo*·re

Shopping

I'd like to buy ...
Vorrei comprare ...　　vo·*ray* kom·*pra*·re ...

I'm just looking.
Sto solo guardando.　　sto *so*·lo gwar·*dan*·do

How much is this?
Quanto costa questo? — kwan·to kos·ta kwe·sto

It's too expensive.
È troppo caro/cara. (m/f) — e tro·po ka·ro/ka·ra

Emergencies

Help!
Aiuto! — a·yoo·to

Call the police!
Chiami la polizia! — kya·mee la po·lee·tsee·a

Call a doctor!
Chiami un medico! — kya·mee oon me·dee·ko

I'm sick.
Mi sento male. — mee sen·to ma·le

I'm lost.
Mi sono perso/persa. (m/f) — mee so·no per·so/per·sa

Where are the toilets?
Dove sono i gabinetti? — do·ve so·no ee ga·bee·ne·tee

Time & Numbers

What time is it?
Che ora è? — ke o·ra e

It's (two) o'clock.
Sono le (due). — so·no le (doo·e)

morning	mattina	ma·tee·na
afternoon	pomeriggio	po·me·ree·jo
evening	sera	se·ra
yesterday	ieri	ye·ree
today	oggi	o·jee
tomorrow	domani	do·ma·nee

1	uno	oo·no
2	due	doo·e
3	tre	tre
4	quattro	kwa·tro
5	cinque	cheen·kwe
6	sei	say
7	sette	se·te
8	otto	o·to
9	nove	no·ve
10	dieci	dye·chee
100	cento	chen·to
1000	mille	mee·le

Transport & Directions

Where's ...?
Dov'è ...? — do·ve ...

What's the address?
Qual'è l'indirizzo? — kwa·le leen·dee·ree·tso

Can you show me (on the map)?
Può mostrarmi (sulla pianta)? — pwo mos·trar·mee (soo·la pyan·ta)

At what time does the ... leave?
A che ora parte ...? — a ke o·ra par·te ...

Does it stop at ...?
Si ferma a ...? — see fer·ma a ...

How do I get there?
Come ci si arriva? — ko·me chee see a·ree·va

bus	l'autobus	low·to·boos
ticket	un biglietto	oon bee·lye·to
timetable	orario	o·ra·ryo
train	il treno	eel tre·no

Behind the Scenes

Send Us Your Feedback

We love to hear from travellers – your comments help make our books better. We read every word, and we guarantee that your feedback goes straight to the authors. Visit **lonelyplanet.com/contact** to submit your updates and suggestions.

Note: We may edit, reproduce and incorporate your comments in Lonely Planet products such as guidebooks, websites and digital products, so let us know if you don't want your comments reproduced or your name acknowledged. For a copy of our privacy policy visit lonelyplanet.com/privacy.

Our Readers

Many thanks to the travellers who used the last edition and wrote to us with helpful hints, useful advice and interesting anecdotes:

Eugenia Bono, Mariasun Garcia, Jacinta Lo Nigro, Carmen Roman, Tim Sansom

Paula's Thanks

Grazie mille to all the fun and fashionable Milanese who spilled the beans on their city: Paola dalla Valentina, Melitta Rodini, Bruno Sacchi, Francesca Giubilei and Claudio Bonacina. Thanks also to Anna Tyler at Lonely Planet. And last, but never least, thanks to Rob for all the laughs along the way.

Acknowledgments

Cover photograph: Galleria Vittorio Emanuele II, Hemis/AWL

Photograph on pp4-5: Galleria Vittorio Emanuele II, Buena Vista Images/Getty

This Book

This 3rd edition of *Pocket Milan & the Lakes* was written by Paula Hardy, with additional research by Belinda Dixon. Paula Hardy also wrote the previous edition and Donna Wheeler wrote the 1st edition.

This guidebook was produced by the following:

Destination Editor Anna Tyler **Coordinating Editor** Susan Paterson **Product Editors** Sarah Billington, Briohny Hooper **Senior Cartographers** Valentina Kremenchutskaya, Anthony Phelan **Book Designer**

Cam Ashley **Assisting Editor** Charlotte Orr **Cover Researcher** Naomi Parker **Thanks to** Ryan Evans, Andi Jones, Claire Murphy, Karyn Noble, Martine Power, Samantha Russell-Tulip, Diana Saengkham, Dianne Schallmeiner, Angela Tinson, Lauren Wellicome, Tony Wheeler

Index

See also separate subindexes for:

⊗ Eating p157

☻ Drinking p158

✪ Entertainment p159

☖ Shopping p159

Our Writers

Paula Hardy

From lakeside *lidos* to annual Furniture Fairs and *spritz*-fuelled *aperitivo* bars, Paula has contributed to Lonely Planet's Italian guides for over 15 years, including previous editions of this guide, *The Italian Lakes*, *Sicily*, *Sardinia* and *Puglia & Basilicata*. When she's not scooting around the *bel paese*, she writes for a variety of travel publications and websites. Currently she divides her time between London, Italy and Morocco, and tweets her finds @paula6hardy

Contributing Writer

Belinda Dixon contributed to Laggo Maggiore and Lago di Como.

Published by Lonely Planet Publications Pty Ltd
ABN 36 005 607 983
3rd edition – Jan 2016
ISBN 978 1 74321 564 7
© Lonely Planet 2016   Photographs © as indicated 2016
10 9 8 7 6 5 4 3 2 1
Printed in China

32953012471134